Favourite
Patron Saints

Favourite Patron Saints

PAUL BURNS

BURNS & OATES
A Continuum imprint
LONDON • NEW YORK

Burns & Oates
A Continuum imprint

The Tower Building   15 East 26th Street
11 York Road   New York
London SE1 7NX   NY 10010

www.continuumbooks.com

First published 2004

British Library Cataloguing-in-Publication Data
A catalogue record for this book is available from the British Library.

ISBN 0-86012-367-7

Illustrations by Penelope Burns

Designed in 10.5/13pt Centaur by Geoff Green Book Design, CB4 5RA
Printed and bound by Cromwell Press Ltd, Trowbridge, Wilts

Contents

Introduction

The cult of saints developed early on in Christianity, and to an extent, saints were 'heroes' similar to those honoured in the Roman Empire. The earliest to be so honoured were martyrs who had shed their blood in defence of their faith. The custom began, with the death of St Polycarp around the middle of the second century, of gathering on the anniversary of the death of a martyr's death. Pagans marked the date of a hero's birth into this world, and to distinguish their form of commemoration, Christians marked the date of 'birth into heaven' – for them the more important world.

By the middle of the third century, faced with systematic persecution, Christians began to attribute special powers to their saints. They became protectors, mirroring the relationship between patron and client in the Roman world. Wealthy Romans protected poorer ones against oppression by such as the taxman in exchange for a lifetime of service. In time it became more attractive, especially for women, to call for help on a distant and dead protector – who might also be a woman – than on an all-too-close and possibly threatening live male protector. So saints became protectors, patrons. Later, when Christianity became the official religion of the empire and the dominant culture of Europe, and all classes, trades and types of person were automatically Christian, saints became more differentiated. Persecution had ended, so there were no more martyrs, and holiness of life became the normal qualification for sainthood. Obviously the apostles and others who had been close to Jesus were early candidates for such honour.

In this process, some saints appeared to be more suitable candidates to act as patrons for specific groups and causes than others, either because of what they had been and done in this life, or because of some story — usually of a marvellous or miraculous nature — that had attached itself to them either during their life and after it. And so it became possible to distinguish patron saints from other saints. And among all patrons, the Virgin Mary became pre-eminent. She, after all, had looked after the physical needs of the young Jesus, so obviously she was ideally placed to look after ours.

As a very rough generalization, during the first millennium, the Church operated through its local cells, from a regional to a parish basis, and patrons served localities. In the second millennium, and especially with the 'discovery' of the New World toward the end of the fifteenth century, the Church became increasingly universal and specialized, with the growth of the religious Orders providing a way of living a holy life and then a multiplicity of means of providing special services to different classes of the needy. So the historical arrangement of this little book shows an increasing proportion of saints from the Orders. St Benedict is the first founder to be so honoured, and for a long time all monks and nuns were Benedictine. Then came the Mendicant Orders in the Middle Ages, the Franciscans and Dominicans, calling the Church back to the poverty of its founder and operating across diocesan and national boundaries. The challenge of the Protestant Reformation produced new Orders, with the Society of Jesus pre-eminent among them, to meet the new requirements of mission. By the nineteenth century, with the industrialization of European and then American society producing all sorts of new needs, Orders multiplied even faster to meet them, and many of their founders have been or are being canonized as saints.

From about the eighteenth century, the 'age of reason', saints began to be seen more as examples and less as intercessors, though they have certainly not lost the latter attribute, especially in cultures where Catholicism has remained the popular culture. The present work stems directly from the tradition of writing about saints begun (in English) by Father Alban Butler at that time. His *Lives* have been re-edited many times since then, most recently in a new one-volume-per-month version published by Burns & Oates and The Liturgical Press between 1993 and 2000, for which I acted as managing editor, as well as revising the January and February volumes. I then produced a one-saint-per-day concise edition of that work, which is the direct source of this book. At the end of that I included a chronological list of its 363 entries by date of death, and this seemed to me an interesting way of arranging the entries here. I have tried to keep roughly a proportionate number for each period in history. As patronages take time to develop, the confines of this work mean excluding a great number of patrons from earlier centuries and perhaps casting about a bit for later ones. But it is designed to be a collection of saints who embody the main requirement for sainthood, 'heroic virtue', rather than just popular patrons for odd aspects of their lives (although one or two of these have been included as they are irresistible). The main source for information on patronages has been Michael Walsh's *Butler's Lives of Patron Saints* (1987), and I gratefully acknowledge the research that went into the production of that volume, as I do the now twice-removed sources provided by the work of the six other revisers who produced the 1993–2000 full edition.

This little gift-book is offered in the hope that it may provide some inspiration (and occasional amusement) for a few minutes a day, either as private reading or perhaps in such a setting as a school assembly, and awaken enough curiosity and interest to encourage at least some readers to move up to the fuller 'Concise' volume – and perhaps even the twelve volumes.

First Millennium

St Mary, the Blessed Virgin

Mother of Jesus, died c. 63
1 January, 15 August and other dates

*Patron of many countries, causes, associations, of which a selection
appears at the foot of this entry*

'Mary, of whom Jesus was born, who is called the Messiah' (Mark 1:16) is the earliest expression of Mary's unique place among the saints. Catholic tradition has always honoured her above all others: if we are Jesus' brothers and sisters, then she is mother to us all.

Luke alone tells of the appearance of the angel Gabriel and her acceptance of the idea that she is to bear a son, even though she is not married. She gives birth to Jesus in a stable 'because there was no place for them in the inn', crowded on account of a census. Matthew tells the story of the family's flight into Egypt and their return, guided by Joseph's* dreams.

The next incident involving her is when Jesus stays behind in the Temple and she upbraids him for treating his parents in this way. Jesus' reply that he has to be 'in my father's house' once more obliges her to accept without understanding. John's Gospel then recounts the story of the wedding at Cana, when she points out to Jesus that the wine has run out. Again Jesus appears to scold her, but he does what she asks. At the end of Jesus' earthly life she stands at the foot of the cross, and from the cross Jesus entrusts her to 'the beloved disciple'. She finally appears briefly in the Acts of the Apostles, with the community at prayer.

Popular devotion was soon supplying more 'details' to flesh out her scant appearances in the New Testament, and by the second century she was venerated as 'Mother of God', the title confirmed in the Greek term *Theotokos* (God-bearer) at the Council of Ephesus in 431; twenty years later the Council of Chalcedon declared that Christ, 'true God and true man' was born of Mary. Devotion to her under a whole series of titles has been constant ever since, though more marked in some traditions than in others. The first day of the year celebrates her as Mother of God, while 15 August is the feast of her 'Assumption' into heaven, a popular belief confirmed as dogma in the Western Church in 1950. The older Eastern tradition refers to her 'Dormition' (falling asleep).

The following list is a selection of her patronages under various titles given to her over the centuries, with dates of formal declarations where applicable:

'Appeared': *Brazil, 1930*

Assumed into Heaven: *France, 1922; French aircrews, 1952; Jamaica, 1951; Paraguay, 1951; South Africa, 1952*

Comforter of the Afflicted: *Luxembourg, 1914*

Faithful Virgin: *Italian police, 1949*

The Immaculate Conception: *Congo, 1891; Equatorial Guinea, 1986; Inner Mongolia, 1914; Spain, 1962; Tanzania, 1984; United States of America, 1847, 1914*

Great Queen of Hungary: *Hungary, 1896*

Mary Immaculate: *Philippines, 1942; Portugal, 1671, 1936*

Mother of Charity: *Cuba, 1917*

Mediatrix of all Graces: *Belgian army chaplains, 1962*

'Most Pure Heart': *Angola, 1984; Central Africa, 1915; Ecuador, 1914*

Mother of Good Counsel: *Albania, 1915*

Our Lady Help of Christians: *Australia and New Zealand, 1916*

Our Lady of the Angels: *Costa Rica, 1914*

    Arabia: *Arabia, 1957*

    Bethlehem: *Spanish architects, 1949*

    Consolation: *pensioners, old people, 1961*

    Coromoto: *Venezuela, 1944*

    Divine Providence: *Puerto Rico, 1969*

    Grace: *motorcyclists, 1947*

    Graces: *Italian skiers, 1955*

    Guadalupe, because of her apparition to Juan Diego (now Blessed) in 1531: *Mexico, 1962; Central and South America, 1962; Peruvian students, 1965*

    Lanka: *Sri Lanka (then Ceylon), 1948*

    Loreto, from the legend that her house flew from Palestine to Loreto in Italy, with a short stopover in former Yugoslavia: *aviation, aircrews, all connected with flying, 1920*

    Lujan: *Argentina, Paraguay, Uruguay, 1920*

    Mercy: *Argentinian army, 1958; Dominican Republic, 1914; Ecuadorian army, 1964*

    Mount Carmel: *Chile, 1923, 1957; Bolivia, 1914; Spanish navy, 1961*

    the Pillar: *Spanish police, 1961*

Patron of India: *India, 1951*

Queen of China: *China, 1941*

Queen of Peace: *civilian war victims, confirmed by Pope John XXIII in around 1960 in recognition of the fact the modern wars killed more civilians than military*

Queen of Poland: *Poland, 1962*

Star of the Sea: *Argentinian navy, 1958*

Emblem: roses or lilies (for purity)

St Joseph

Husband of Mary, died in first century
19 March and 1 May

Austria; Belgium; Bohemia; Canada; Mexico; 'New Spain'; Peru; Russia;
carpenters; doubters; travellers; house-hunters; happy death; the universal Church;
all workers; missions to China, and others

Joseph is a shadowy figure in the Gospels, mentioned only by Matthew and Luke. Mary is 'engaged' to him when the angel tells her she is to have a son, and Matthew makes clear that the baby is not his. His reaction is that of a 'righteous' man: not to shame her but to break off the engagement.

His subsequent actions are guided by dreams: he is told that the child is 'from the Holy Spirit' and so marries Mary; he is told to take her and the infant Jesus to Egypt to hide from Herod's jealousy at the coming of another 'king'; then he is told when it is safe to take them back to Israel. This rather passive, if honourable, part is the only one he plays in the Gospels.

Nevertheless, he was presumably a central figure in Jesus' early life, and so Christians from an early age wanted to know more about him. Later, 'apocryphal' (doubtful or invented) accounts supplied from imagination what history had not recorded. He became an older man, a widower (to explain 'Jesus' brothers'), and by the Middle Ages, as a deceived husband, he had become something of a figure of fun.

As devotion to the humanity of Christ (as opposed to his divinity) increased, the Holy Family became an object of veneration, and Joseph was treated with greater respect. He also became the 'helper' above all others for those in various needs, as he had provided for the needs of Jesus and Mary.

His patronage of carpenters (and allied trades) is traditional, following the Gospel account; of doubters is because he doubted whether to take Mary as his wife; of travellers and house-hunters is based on the flight into Egypt and the difficulty finding a room in Bethlehem; of a happy death is traditional, based on the supposition that he died with Jesus and Mary at his bedside.

Missionary Orders spread devotion to him around the world in the sixteenth century, and in 1678 he was officially proclaimed patron of missions to the Chinese. He was declared patron of the universal Church in 1870, on the grounds that he had been head of the Holy Family. In 1956 he was declared the 'exemplar and protector' of Christian workers, venerated on the feast of St Joseph the Worker on 1 May. This was instituted as a deliberate move to give a Christian slant to 'socialist' (then feared as virtually 'communist') Labour Day.

He was declared patron of Mexico, 'New Spain' and the Philippines in 1555, of Canada in 1624, Bohemia in 1665 and Austria in 1675; Pope Pius XI made him a 'special protector' of Russia – against Soviet 'outrages' – in 1930; his patronage of South Vietnam, however, declared in 1952, failed to prevent it falling to the communists; he was made principal patron of Peru in 1957.

Emblems: carpenter's tools; a lily (for his chastity)

St Stephen

Martyr, died in 36
26 December

Deacons; stonemasons and, by extension, all those involved
in the building trades

Stephen is the first recorded martyr and generally accepted as the first of Jesus' followers to die. He is also the first deacon listed among the seven chosen from the Jews living outside Palestine to help the apostles with the extra work resulting from increased conversions. 'A man full of faith and the Holy Spirit', he and the other six were brought before the apostles, who laid their hands on them. The account of this and of Stephen's subsequent fate is in Chapters 6 and 7 of the Acts of the Apostles.

The 'wonders and signs' Stephen produced earned him the jealousy of a certain group, who encouraged others to delate him to the council for blasphemy and subversion of the Judaic faith. His judges, even though they saw that he had 'the face of an angel', challenged him to justify himself. In a long speech, Stephen told them how their scriptures showed them that, from Moses to Jesus, God was always moving his people on to something new, showing them not to put their trust in 'houses made of stone'.

This message was not acceptable to the priests, the guardians of the 'stone' tradition embodied in the Temple. They 'ground their teeth' at Stephen, who told them he had seen 'the glory of God and Jesus standing at the right hand of God'. This was the final insult, and they dragged him out of the city and began to stone him. They had clearly planned this in advance; it was no spontaneous lynching but a judicial execution, indicated by the fact that they had brought witnesses, who 'laid their cloaks at the feet of a young man named Saul' – the first appearance of the future St Paul.*

Stephen was venerated in both East and West from around the fourth century, when renewed persecution made Christians look back to their early 'martyrs' – meaning witnesses.

He is patron of deacons because he led the first group of them; of stonemasons, and by extension, all those involved in the building trades, obviously because of the manner of his death – a patronage dating from the Middle Ages. He is also invoked against headaches, which might seem a rather sick joke.

Emblems: stones and a palm branch (the general emblem of martyrdom)

St James the Greater

Apostle and martyr, died c. 44
25 July

Guatemala; Nicaragua; Spain

This James, the older of the two apostles with the same
name, was called by Jesus, with his brother John, immediately after Peter* and Andrew.* These two brothers, the sons of
Zebedee, nicknamed *Boanerges* ('sons of thunder') by Jesus,
form a privileged trio with Peter in the New Testament narratives. They witness the raising of Jairus' daughter and the transfiguration of Jesus, and are later called to keep watch during
Jesus' agony in the garden (which they fail to do).

Matthew's Gospel has their ambitious mother asking for
one son to sit on either side of Jesus in the kingdom of heaven;
Mark has them making the request themselves, to which Jesus
replies by asking them if they can drink the same cup as he:
meaning being put to death. They reply that they can, and
James was in fact the first of the apostles to be martyred. The
Acts of the Apostles tells that 'King Herod [Agrippa] ... had
James, the brother of John, killed with the sword.' Tradition
claims that his body was buried in Jerusalem.

Eight centuries later he emerged as the hero of the reconquest
of Spain from the Moors, *Santiago matamoros*, 'James the Moorslayer'. One (most improbable) legend has it that he preached
in Spain, another that his remains were moved there, that an
angel later led a shepherd to discover his bones at Compostela,
'the field of stars', through stars shining down on a spot in

Galicia, in the north-western corner of the Iberian peninsula, from where he led the Christian forces as a mounted knight. As a result, Santiago de Compostela became one of the three great pilgrimage destinations of medieval and modern Europe.

He has been patron of Spain, because of his role in the reconquest, since the ninth century. The pilgrim routes to Compostela have recently been restored, and many thousands each year walk, ride, cycle or drive 'the road to Santiago'. On his feast-day, a six-foot-high censer, the *botafumeiro*, hung from the crossing vault, swings in a great arc across the transepts of Santiago Cathedral. Guatemala and Nicaragua share him as patron from official decrees in 1914.

Emblems: the traditional pilgrim's staff; wallet; and scallop shell

St Paul

Apostle and martyr, died 64 or 65

25 January and 29 June

Malta; Greece; the Cursillo *movement and all forms of Catholic Action
or lay apostolate*

T he 'young man named Saul' met Christ on the road to
Damascus in the most famous conversion story of all
time. Celebrated on 25 January, the feast of his conversion now
closes the Week of Prayer for Christian Unity. His subsequent
story as Paul is related in the Acts of the Apostles and can
be glimpsed from his own letters to the early Christian
communities.

He was born in Tarsus in about 4 BC and learned his devout
Jewish faith from the great rabbi Gamaliel. He approved of the
stoning of Stephen, but after his conversion he withdrew to the
desert to pray, and then joined Peter in Jerusalem for a time,
after which he embarked on a travelling missionary apostolate.
In the year 49 he returned to Jerusalem, and in the discussion
known as the Council of Jerusalem he persuaded Peter* that
Gentiles (non-Jews) could be converted to the new Christian
faith without having to embrace Judaism first. This great turning-
point changed the fledgling Church from a local movement
into one that spread into the dominant cultures of classical
Greece and Rome.

He journeyed throughout the eastern and central Mediter-
ranean region, preaching and writing to his converts. His
remarkable letters provided the doctrinal basis of the emergent

Church and, indeed, the subject matter for most later theology. He preaches Christ crucified and raised from the dead: a message of love for all that must inform the Christian way of life.

Back in Jerusalem, he was threatened by a hostile mob and used his Roman citizenship to appeal for protective custody. He was taken to Rome, where after some years under a lenient form of house arrest he was tried for 'anti-imperial' activities and beheaded – traditionally on the same day as St Peter, 29 June in the year 64 or 65.

His patronage of the *Cursillo* movement, for lay people, which originated in Spain, was confirmed by Pope Paul VI in 1973 and, by implication, extended to all forms of lay apostolate. The New Testament describes his visit to Greece and his shipwreck on Malta; both celebrate feasts of his 'arrival', and his patronage of Greece was confirmed in 1914 and of Malta in 1962.

Emblem: a sword and a book, for his activity and his writing; in art he tends to be shown as elderly and slight, with a long beard

St Peter

Apostle, bishop and martyr, died 64 or 65
29 June

Fishermen

Peter's original name was Simon, but Jesus called him *Cephas,* a Greek word for 'rock'; *Petros (Petra* in Latin) is another, so he became Peter, or Simon Peter, the rock: 'You are Peter and upon this rock [*tu es Petrus et super hanc petram*] I will build my Church.'

He came from Bethsaida in Galilee and was Andrew's* brother, working with him, and James* and John, the sons of Zebedee, as a fisherman. Jesus called out to them to follow him, to be made 'fishers of men', and they immediately left their nets and went with him. Peter becomes a leader among the disciples and is shown as enthusiastic, questioning and impulsive, with a streak of weakness indicated by his triple denial after Jesus' arrest. After his resurrection Jesus asks him to state his love three times, and gives him the commission to 'feed my lambs ... feed my lambs ... feed my sheep'.

After Pentecost he is the first to address the crowds, who are amazed at the transformation from the cowed group hiding in an upper room. He attributes the change to God's Spirit, whose presence 'you see and hear'. After working cures and other signs, he left James in charge of the Church in Jerusalem and embarked on a series of missionary journeys. He was arrested by King Herod Agrippa and dramatically rescued, apparently through the intervention of an angel. He went to

Antioch in Asia Minor, to Corinth in Greece, and finally to Rome, capital of the empire, where he was martyred during the persecution under Nero (emperor from 54 to 68). The story that he asked to be crucified head down, so as not to imitate Jesus, dates from the early third century, by which time his name was always placed first on lists of Bishops of Rome.

He is traditionally patron of fishermen on account of the description of his calling in the New Testament. In the Middle Ages he was invoked by many other groups with less obvious connections to his life.

Emblem: keys, as Jesus gave him 'the keys to the kingdom of heaven'; in art he is portrayed as strongly built, with a short, square beard

St Andrew

Apostle, died in first century
30 November

Scotland; Russia; fishermen

S imon Peter's* brother Andrew was called with him to 'fish for people' (as newer translations put it) in the three 'synoptic' Gospels. John's gives a different account of his calling, making him a disciple of John the Baptist,* who points Jesus out to them as the 'Lamb of God', whereupon Andrew goes to find his brother and tells him, 'We have found the Messiah.' This is a more careful theological account than the simpler one given in the other three Gospels.

It is Andrew who tells Jesus, when some 5,000 people sit down to listen to him, expecting also to be fed, that there is a boy with 'five barley loaves and two fishes', asking what that amounts to among so many people. He later gives Jesus Philip's message that some Greeks wish to speak to him, to which Jesus responds rather enigmatically with the saying about a grain of wheat having to fall to the ground and die if it is to produce fruit.

Andrew is not mentioned after Pentecost, but the church historian Eusebius claims that he preached in Greece. Where and how he died is not known, and the tradition that he was crucified on an X-shaped cross is not found before the tenth century. His status as 'first-called' among the apostles gave him huge appeal, and most of his supposed relics were enshrined in

Constantinople in 356 or 357 to give the new capital of the empire a prestige to rival Rome's.

He became patron of Scotland through the story of a 'St Regulus' (the name meaning 'rule') being told by an angel to take Andrew's remaining relics 'to the ends of the earth' – and where else could this mean but Scotland? He has been somewhat supplanted there by more war-like leaders such as Wallace, but the 1321 Declaration of Arbroath, an appeal by the Scots to the pope to help put an end to the violence being done to them by the English, called upon 'the most gentle Saint Andrew' to keep the Scottish people under his protection for ever.

His patronage of Russia (which he shares with St Joseph* and St Basil) derives from a baseless legend that he preached there. That of fishermen stems, like his brother's, from the Gospels.

Emblems: X-shaped cross (*saltire* in heraldry); fishhook

St John the Baptist

Died in first century
24 June and 29 August

Florence; farriers; tailors; spas; motorways

John the Baptist occupies an unusual place among saints, since he is not a 'follower of Christ' but the 'forerunner of Christ'. He is also exceptionally honoured with two feast days, one commemorating his birth on 24 June, with 'St John's Eve' celebrations echoing those of the summer solstice, and the other his death, on 29 August.

Luke alone tells the story of his conception following a message from the angel Gabriel, which leaves his father Zechariah struck dumb with disbelief in view of his mother's age. His mother, Elizabeth, is a 'relative' of Mary* the mother of Jesus, who sets out to visit her (an event celebrated in the Church's calendar on 31 May), so John and Jesus are spoken of as cousins.

John next appears preaching a message of conversion and repentance in the desert, dressed in camel hair, with a leather belt, and eating wild locusts and honey. He proclaimed a time of universal judgement, which he called 'the kingdom of God'. Jesus came to him for baptism, even though he had nothing of which to repent.

John rebuked Herod Antipas for his evil life, especially his latest – tenth – marriage, to Herodias, who had been his brother's wife and was also his niece, in violation of Jewish Law. Herodias persuaded Herod to have him arrested. The news reached Jesus, who may have seen it as a threat to him too, as he 'withdrew to Galilee', where he continued to preach John's message of repentance. The New Testament then provides the colourful story of Herodias' daughter Salome dancing before Herod and pleasing him so much that he offers her anything she asks for. Her mother then prompts her to ask for the head of John the Baptist on a plate.

The Jewish historian Josephus is more circumspect and says only that Herod had John put to death for political reasons. He preached near the Dead Sea and may have been associated with the Qumran community, which the Dead Sea Scrolls show as preaching the same message of repentance and baptism.

He is patron of farriers perhaps because he seems to need shoes; of tailors because he wore 'clothing of camel's hair' (Matt. 3.4); of Florence for reasons unknown; of spas for the health-giving water of baptism; of motorways (unofficially) for preaching 'Make straight the way of the Lord' (John 1.23).

Emblem: lamb and cross, as he said, 'Here is the Lamb of God' (John 1.29)

St Martha

Disciple, died in first century

29 July

Housewives; servants; hoteliers; waiters and waitresses

In Luke's Gospel (Chapter 10), Jesus goes into a house occupied by two sisters, Martha and Mary. Mary sits at his feet and listens to him, while Martha, 'distracted by her many tasks', asks Jesus to tell her to come and lend a hand. Jesus, though, tells her that Mary 'has chosen the better part, which will not be taken away from her'. And so the qualitative distinction between contemplative and active life was born, and 'a Martha' became a dismissive term.

In John's – later and more overtly theological – Gospel (Chapter 11), however, Martha comes into her own in the account of the raising of Lazarus. It is she who tells Jesus that if he had come sooner her brother would not have died. Jesus, who had delayed his visit until he knew Lazarus had died, tells her that he will rise again, which she takes to mean on the last day and says she knows that. But no, Jesus says, 'I am the resurrection and the life', and he asks her if she believes this. Her reply is, 'Yes, Lord, I believe that you are the Messiah, the Son of God, the one coming into the world.' For this confession of faith, she is commemorated first on 29 July, with Mary and Lazarus sharing her 'memorial'.

We may conjecture that Martha and Mary, along with other women disciples, were present at the Last Supper, with Martha responsible for the cooking, perhaps helped by Jesus' mother but probably not by her sister Mary. Neither sister nor their brother is recorded as playing any part in the young Church after Jesus' resurrection. Tradition in the East puts the three in a leaking boat, which reached Cyprus (where the women disappear and the man becomes a bishop); in the West they are also put in a boat, which reaches Marseilles, where Martha disappears, Mary (confused with Mary Magdalene*) lives in her cave as the repentant sinner, and Lazarus (confused with the poor man in the parable of Dives and Lazarus) of course becomes the bishop.

Martha's patronages are traditional and an obvious outcome of Luke's story. In 1963 she was officially decreed patron of Italian hoteliers, hotel staff, and waiters and waitresses. She acts on both householder and servant level and was held up by Pope Paul VI, when he confirmed the decree in 1973 as an example of the hospitality we should all show, receiving guests 'kindly and humanely'.

St Mary Magdalene

Disciple, died first century

22 July

Repentant prostitutes

Mary Magdalene (meaning 'from Magdala') has a long history in Western art and folklore as the repentant prostitute, but she deserves better. This identification stems from the fact that her first appearance in Luke's Gospel (8.1–3), when she is described as having been cured of 'evil spirits', follows the story of the woman 'who was a sinner', who anoints Jesus and dries his feet with her hair. In fact what the Gospels tell us about her make her a significant figure without her attendant legends.

A group of women, as well as 'the twelve', accompanies Jesus in his itinerant ministry. Mary is named first among them, and 'seven demons had gone out' from her. The number seven indicates completeness, so this means that she was completely in the grip of, and then completely cured of, some grave psychological disorder. The women stay with Jesus through crises when male disciples abandon him, and are with him right through to his crucifixion and burial.

Mary is singled out from the others by her visit to the tomb on Easter morning. In John's account, she finds the stone rolled back and runs to tell Peter that 'they' have taken the Lord away. She returns to the tomb and stays there weeping. She sees a figure she takes for the gardener and asks him if he knows where Jesus' body has been taken. He answers simply by speaking her name, whereupon she recognizes him, thus becoming the first person to be given the gift of faith in the risen Christ. He tells her to go and tell the disciples, which she does, but they (according to Luke) find this 'an idle tale' – because it was told by a woman. Matthew and Mark tell basically the same story, with Mary Magdalene the one person who features in all four accounts. So she can be called 'apostle to the apostles'.

After that she passes into legend, claimed mainly by France, where she is supposed to have sailed to Provence (a confusion with Martha's* sister Mary) and died at Saint-Maximin after living there in a cave, clad only in her hair, eventually being buried at Vézelay in Burgundy.

She is patron of reformed prostitutes because of her identification with the woman 'who was a sinner' – male imagination presumably regarding this as the most likely form of female sin, though the Gospel account gives no justification for this.

Emblems: jar of ointment; open book; boat; long flowing hair; skull, for repentance

St Thomas

Apostle, died first century
3 July

India and Pakistan; architects, builders, Italian quantity surveyors; blind people

Thomas makes just three brief appearances as an individual in the Gospels, but one of them is the familiar story of 'doubting Thomas'.

He is not with the other disciples hiding fearfully in a locked house after the crucifixion, when Jesus appears among them and shows them his wounds as proof that it is the Jesus who was crucified who is now the risen Christ. The others tell Thomas that they have seen the Lord, but he replies that until he can put his finger into the marks of the nails in Jesus' hands and feet, and his hand into the wound made by the lance in his side, he will not believe.

A week later he is with the others in the same place. Jesus again appears, and he tells Thomas to do just what he had said. This is enough for Thomas, who exclaims, 'My Lord and my God', thus becoming the first apostle to make a full confession of faith in Christ's divinity.

Before that, he proposes to go to Lazarus' house 'and die with him'. At the Last Supper he is the questioner who elicits Jesus' statement 'I am the way, the truth, and the life.' His few brief appearances are thus of considerable importance for the development of faith.

Nothing is really known about his subsequent life and death, but tradition takes him to the East, as far as southern

India, where the Syriac Christians of Malabar still call themselves 'Christians of St Thomas'. They claim that he was martyred there in the year 72 and buried at Mylapore, near Madras. The earliest versions of this tradition date from the third century, but there is no doubt that when Western explorers (and then colonizers) reached India later, they found established Christian communities there.

In the 1940s Coptic manuscripts of the documents known as *The Gospel of Thomas* and *The Infancy Gospel of Thomas* were discovered. These ancient 'apocryphal' gospels are largely concerned with pointless miracles attributed to Jesus, but the discovery increased devotion to Thomas in the West, and the Vatican appeared to endorse the Indian tradition by moving his feast-day from the traditional 21 December to the date of his death claimed in the Malabar tradition.

He is (informally) patron of India and Pakistan because of this tradition. His patronage of builders, architects and (1955) Italian quantity surveyors derives from a story in *The Gospel of Thomas*, repeated in the medieval *Golden Legend*, that he built a palace for a local king in India. He is invoked by blind people because of his 'spiritual blindness' in refusing to believe without seeing: 'None so blind as those who will not see.'

St Justin Martyr

Martyr, c. 100–65
1 June

Philosophers and philosophy; apologists

J ustin lived at a time when the early Church was seeking to justify its beliefs to the pagan thinkers of Greece and Rome. He was a Greek and studied philosophy in a search for 'the vision of God'. He examined and rejected the Stoic, Peripatetic and Pythagorean schools, then found some comfort in Platonism. It was, however, only a chance (or divinely planned?) meeting with an old man, who told him about the Hebrew prophets and Christianity, that he was convinced of having found 'a sure and useful philosophy'.

He was probably about 30 years of age when he became a Christian, and he then became the first significant Christian philosopher and 'apologist' – the term applied to those who produced 'apologies', arguments, for the Christian faith against the Roman religion of many gods; Judaism, which did not recognize Christ as Son of God or Messiah; and Gnosticism, which claimed esoteric knowledge about God and the material world. He travelled to Rome in about 150 and there established a school of philosophy.

He was fearless in proclaiming his faith and the reasons for it, which made him many enemies. Refusal to sacrifice to the Roman gods was punishable by death, which he accepted readily as a means to salvation. Together with six other Christians, he was beheaded in about 165. Two of his major works from among many survive, known as the *Apologies* and the *Dialogue with Trypho* (a Jew whom he met shortly after his conversion). It is in this that he gives an account of earlier searches for the truth. His original contribution to Christian thinking is the theory that before Christ pagans were given 'seeds' of divine reason, which was fully revealed in Christ, 'the Word'. He also provides the most complete guide to Christian belief and practice in the second century.

His patronages are traditional, following logically from his life, and have not been officially confirmed.

St Laurence

Martyr, died 258

10 August

Cooks; librarians

L aurence is one of the most venerated of all martyrs, but essentially all that is known of his life and death is that he was one of Rome's seven deacons and that he was killed in an intensification of persecution under Emperor Valerian (253–60).

Pope Sixtus I, consecrated in 257, was arrested while addressing a congregation in the cemetery of Praetextatus on 6 August the following year. He, four subdeacons and two deacons were executed on the spot; Laurence was also there and was arrested but not executed until four days later. The probable means of his death was the traditional sword-thrust to the neck.

After that, legend takes over. The deacons were responsible for the Church's goods and for almsgiving. When Sixtus warned Laurence of his impending death, the story goes, Laurence sold the sacred vessels he was responsible for (but not the books) and gave the proceeds to the poor. When he was asked to produce the Church's 'treasures', he paraded the poor, the sick and widows before the Prefect, telling him these were the Church's treasure. For this he was condemned to a slow death, and this is where the gridiron comes in – helped, perhaps, by a missing 'p' in a scribe's account, leaving *assus est* ('He was roasted') from *passus est* ('He suffered').

The gridiron seems to have been borrowed from the story of the martyrdom of St Vincent of Zaragoza and made Laurence's story especially popular in Spain, though veneration of him spread all over Europe. King Philip II of Spain (1556–98) built his great monastery/palace, St Laurence of the Escorial, on a gridiron plan in his honour.

He is (unofficial) patron of cooks because he asked to be turned over when one side was done and told the onlookers they could eat his body when the whole of it was 'done to a turn'. He is also (with the legendary Catherine of Alexandria – where there was a famous library) patron of librarians for refusing to sell the books in his care.

St Valentine

Martyr, died possibly third century
14 February

Lovers

Valentine is another martyr who has become a famous patron on the basis of very little fact. Until recently there seemed to be two Valentines: one a martyr in Rome, the other a bishop of Terni, some 60 miles to the north, also apparently killed in Rome. Now the Vatican appears to have accepted that the Roman martyr is the true one.

We know more about his cult than we do about his life and death. A basilica was built in his honour, possibly by the year 350, on the spot where he is supposed to have been martyred, 'on the via Flaminia by the Milvan Bridge' (where Constantine won his victory over Maxentius, ensuring toleration for Christianity throughout the Roman Empire and its eventual adoption as the official religion). Pope Paschal I later transferred his remains to a special chapel he had built on to the church of St Praxedes.

How did he become patron of lovers? There are various explanations.

He was (if any of his story is actual fact) killed on the Roman festival of Lupercalia, when boys drew names of girls they fancied, and his association with lovers might be an attempt to make this day less 'heathen, lewd and superstitious' (as Fr Butler called it).

His feast day is, apparently, according to Chaucer, the time when birds choose their mates, but Chaucer may have been referring to the betrothal of King Richard II to Anne of Bohemia on 3 May 1381. This would suggest that he is perhaps the wrong Valentine, and the patron should really be a bishop of Genoa of the same name, whose feast-day is 2 May.

Whatever the reason, the card and flower industries now have more reason to be grateful for his (possible) life and death than any others do to any other patron. This is a relatively recent revival of an old custom. In the 1950s, difficult though this is to credit now, it could be referred to as 'hardly more than a memory'.

St George

Martyr, died 303
23 April

England; Catalonia; Portugal; Genoa; Istanbul; Venice;
the Order of the Garter; Italian cavalry

Confusion and offence were rife in England when St George was 'demoted' in the Church's calendar reform of 1969. There were dread rumours that he had been declared non-existent, but this was not the case; he was simply, with many others, removed from the 'universal' category, meaning veneration *should* be paid to him, to the 'local'; meaning veneration *could* be paid by national churches. It was not quite the national humiliation at the hands of the (European!) papacy that was suspected.

He was almost certainly a genuine martyr, executed at Lydda (now Lod in Israel) during the persecution under Diocletian, which was more severe in the East, in 303. It was not until some 200 years later that fabulous 'acts' describing his martyrdom began to circulate widely. These became extraordinarily popular, even before the medieval introduction of the slaying of the dragon, though their obviously fabulous and exaggerated character also made them widely mistrusted.

He emerged as one of the greatest 'protectors' of all time: first as a protector of the armies of Byzantium, probably because the 'acts' describe him as an officer in the Roman army. His fame in the West increased after he and St Demetrius 'appeared' to crusaders at the siege of Antioch in 1098, thus becoming known as 'the martyr knights'.

King Richard I of England placed himself and his armies under his protection. His feast-day was made a national festival after the Battle of Agincourt in 1415, and he was formally named Protector of England by Pope Benedict XIV.

The Order of the Garter was founded in 1348 by King Edward III, who named George as its patron, which he has been ever since.

He was officially decreed a patron of Istanbul in 1914.

The Italian cavalry have long had a devotion to him, and asked that he be declared their patron in 1937; this was granted, with the pope remarking that he was by then protecting soldiers in armoured cars rather than on horses, and confirmed by Pope Pius XII in 1956.

St Antony of Egypt

Abbot, about 251–356
17 January

Basket-makers; butchers; brush-makers; domestic animals; invoked against skin diseases

Antony became the inspiration for generations of monks through the popularity of his Life, written by St Athanasius (295–373), of which copies were to be found in most medieval libraries.

The best known of the Fathers, or *abbas*, of the Egyptian desert, he gave away all his possessions in literal obedience to the Gospel and lived as a hermit in the desert for twenty years. He then began to found monasteries, collections of huts in which monks lived as hermits. After this he retired to the top of a mountain, where disciples followed him, asking for a 'word of wisdom' or 'wise saying'. These sayings of his and of many later 'abbots' who followed his lifestyle were collected and are still widely published.

His message was 'flight from the world'. This was achieved physically, by voluntary flight to the deserts (into which Christians had previously been driven by persecution). It was also metaphorical, with the world of one's body representing one's temptations and 'the desert' a symbol of resisting them in one's own mind – hence all later representation of 'The Temptations of St Antony'. 'Demons' are strongest when one is alone, and so if they can be conquered in solitude, the victory is the greater.

He appears truly to have lived to the age of about 105, perhaps a tribute to a moderate diet and a dry climate, and was first buried secretly on his mountain. His remains were taken later to Alexandria and then to Constantinople, and were claimed by France in the Middle Ages. There he started a second career as a healer, when two noblemen claimed to have been cured of ergotism (a disease caught from eating infected rye bread, causing painful burning rashes and delirium) through his intercession, and founded the Hospital Brothers of St Antony in gratitude. In the thirteenth century, when the disease was at its height, these 'Hospitallers' were running some 360 hospitals. They wore cloaks with a T-shaped cross on them, rang bells to announce their arrival on missions, and kept pigs with bells round their necks; they, rather than his life, are the source of most of his patronages and emblems.

Antony kept himself from idleness in the desert by weaving rush mats and baskets, and this accounts for the one patronage that derives from his life, that of basket-makers. That of domestic animals comes from the pigs the Hospitallers kept, and those of butchers and brush-makers (from hogshair bristle) from the same source. His fame as a healer of ergotism led to his being invoked against all forms of skin disease.

Emblems: T-cross, known as *Tau*, representing a walking stick or staff for his great age; a bell in his hand, a pig by his side, a pig with a bell round its neck; a book, for his sayings; flames or a devil, for his supposed temptations

St Monica

332–87

27 August

Mothers; wives

Whether the mother of the great St Augustine is the ideal patron for mothers may be open to question, but there is no doubting the vital part each played in the life of the other. She is certainly not an example of 'hands-off' parenting, and her story is inextricably linked to his. Augustine tells it with complete honesty in his *Confessions*, rendering her a most vivid figure in comparison with most saints' mothers. As a wife, less is told of her, but her main virtue seems to have been patience.

She was born in North Africa, in what is now Algeria. Her parents were Christian, but she was married young to a pagan named Patricius, whose only significant contribution seems to have been to have given her children. Three of these survived past infancy, but there is no record of whether Augustine's brother and sister gave their mother as much trouble as he did. Bad company as a student in Carthage was the start, followed by a mistress (to whom he was at least faithful for fifteen years) and embracing Manichaeism, not orthodox Christianity. Monica prayed for his reform in faith and morals.

By 328 Augustine was a famous teacher and decided to move to Italy. Monica was determined to come with him (Patricius being by now conveniently dead), but being mothered was not part of his plan, and he tricked her into believing he was just going to look at the port … Some time later, though, she did follow him – to Milan. Augustine was depressed and seeking consolation in another mistress, then an engagement, and finally a vow of celibacy. Monica came to the rescue and kept house for him, his son (whom his first mistress had left with him when she returned to Carthage, no doubt in some anger), his brother and some friends.

At that time St Ambrose (c. 340–97) was archbishop of Milan. Monica was deeply influenced by him and probably played a part in Augustine's decision to seek baptism from him in 387. His conversion and baptism brought her deep joy. When he tired of teaching and decided to return to North Africa, she went with him. Before embarking at the Roman port of Ostia, the two had a deep and peaceful spiritual conversation. This, she said, satisfied her deepest desires and she saw no point in going further. In fact, she was already mortally ill, and she died at Ostia within a few days.

Her patronages are traditional, dating from the Middle Ages, when her cult as a saint began.

St Martin of Tours

Bishop, about 336–97

11 November

Italian and French soldiers; horses and horse-riders; beggars; wine-growers; geese

Like Antony,* Martin became one of the best-known saints of the Middle Ages through the popularity of a book about him. This was written by Sulpicius Severus and is a truly contemporary account, finished a year before Martin died. It follows the principle that a saint should be as much like Jesus as possible, so Martin's life is made to follow the Gospel pattern quite closely. This became a model for later Lives of saints, so that Martin might be seen as the typical saint.

He came from a pagan family in central Europe and became a soldier, like his father, in the Roman imperial army. He was posted to northern France and was drawn to Christianity, which would make it impossible for him to fight. On a cold winter's night, outside Amiens, he saw a beggar shivering and cut his own cloak in two, giving half to the beggar. That night Christ appeared to him in a dream, saying Martin had 'covered him with his garment'. He was baptized and, with some difficulty, left the army. He was encouraged by St Hilary of Poitiers, and was instructed enough to preach against Arianism.

After a visit to his homeland, he returned by way of Milan, where the Arian bishop had him exiled to a small island. He eventually rejoined Hilary, who had also been exiled for a time. He felt a vocation to a hermit's life, and Hilary gave him some land; others then followed him, and he set up what is considered to be the earliest monastic community in France (then Gaul). After ten years the people of Tours wanted to elect him as their bishop and tricked him into the city by telling him a sick man there needed his care.

As bishop, he continued to live as simply as he had as a monk. He travelled widely, setting up rural parishes, an innovation at the time. He founded a great abbey at Marmoutier, where he established the first seminary to train priests. He disputed with an ascetic group known as Priscillianists after their leader, Priscillian, and condemned them as heretics. As tended to happen, a doctrinal dispute then involved the secular powers, who had Priscillian and some followers executed. Martin, though not responsible, was to feel guilty about this for the rest of his life.

After his death, Tours became one the foremost pilgrim destinations, and remained so until the sixteenth century. The story of his dividing his cloak became a popular subject for representation in stained glass, statues and paintings.

His patronage of Italian infantry was formally granted in 1951 and extended to French infantry the following year. Both stem from his profession of soldier. He is usually shown riding a horse when he divided his cloak for the beggar, and this led cavalrymen also to seek his patronage, extending to all riders and their horses. The seemingly unconnected patronages of geese and winegrowers derive from his feast-day falling around the time geese migrate and the wine harvest is completed.

St John Chrysostom

Bishop and Doctor, about 350–407
13 September

Istanbul; preachers, sacred eloquence and oratory

John was born in Antioch, and was well educated by his
mother, followed by further studies in scripture, doctrine
and law. He joined a group of hermits living in community in
the mountains when he was 23. His damp cave did his health
no good, and after seven years he returned to Antioch, where
he was ordained and given special charge of the poor of the
diocese.

His fame spread through a series of sermons, and in 397 the
emperor made him archbishop (or patriarch) of Constantinople. He set about imposing drastically austere reforms on his
household and the clergy, who resented them, and he called the
Empress Eudoxia 'a Jezebel', to which she responded by erecting
a silver statue of herself in front of his cathedral and organizing
games around it. In 402 quarrels with the patriarch of Alexandria, Theophilus, led to his exile from Constantinople after an
encounter known as the Oak Tree Synod, at which he was effectively 'ambushed' by supporters of Theophilus and Eudoxia. But
the people demanded his return, and a convenient earthquake
put the fear of God into Eudoxia and her supporters.

Back in his see, he made no attempt to ingratiate himself,
resumed his attacks on the empress, and was again banished by
the machinations of Theophilus, leading to a riot during which
his cathedral church of Santa Sophia was burned. John's faith-

ful helper Olympias, a great heiress who had helped him build churches, was falsely accused of starting the fire and also exiled. John wrote to her from his place of exile in Armenia; seventeen of his letters to her have survived, but none of her replies. He also wrote copious complaints to the pope, who did nothing practical to free him. He was then forced to walk several hundred miles in bad weather, and this brought about his death. He was soon recognized as a saint and declared a Father of the Church at the Council of Chalcedon in 433.

He was proclaimed a Doctor of the Church by Pope Pius V in the sixteenth century. *Chrysostom* means 'golden-mouthed' and he is a natural choice for patron of preachers and orators. This was officially confirmed in 1884 and again in 1908. As patriarch of Constantinople (now Istanbul) he is also a natural patron of the city, and this was confirmed in 1914.

St Jerome

Doctor, c. 325–420
30 September

Scripture scholars

J erome came from a wealthy family north of Venice and was sent to Rome to study Greek and Latin. After three years travelling around western Europe in search of further knowledge and experience he underwent a conversion and decided to become a monk. A powerful character with a quick temper, he quarrelled with some of his community and moved to Antioch. There he was seriously ill and in a delirious dream saw Christ, who accused him of being more attached to the classics, especially to Cicero, than he was to him.

He withdrew to a desert region south of Antioch and began to study Hebrew, which he hated. Four years later he was ordained priest in Antioch and then moved to Constantinople to study the scriptures. He began to translate some Church Fathers and to write commentaries on books of the Bible. Going to Rome as an interpreter, he was retained as secretary by Pope Damasus, and decided to undertake a complete translation of the Bible from Hebrew and Greek into Latin.

He brought the ascetic spirit of the desert with him to Rome and began to attack vain women and worldly priests, which could have resulted in his being driven from the city, but he was protected by a group of devout women who attached themselves to him and studied the scriptures with him – some of them mastering Hebrew better than he. This association led to rumours that he and one of them, Paula, were lovers and proba-bly prevented him from being elected pope when Damasus died. He firmly stated that Paula and her daughter, Eustochium, were 'mine in Christ, whether the world likes it or not'.

He left Rome again and went back to the Holy Land, fol-lowed later by his women disciples. After studying monasticism in Egypt, they settled near Jerusalem, Jerome in a cave, the women in three communities nearby, and went on with the work of translating the Bible, which became the Vulgate, on which all Catholic translations had to be based until the late twentieth century. This was his great legacy to the Church, for which he is venerated as a Doctor of the Church.

He was formally declared patron of all who study the scrip-tures in 1920, on the 1,500th anniversary of his death.

Emblems: a stone or a skull, for his presumed penitential life in his cave; in art he is often shown with a lion at his feet, but the legend behind this, that he took a thorn out of its paw, is borrowed from St Gerasimus; he is also shown as a cardinal, on account of his closeness to Pope Damasus, but there were no cardinals in his time

St Patrick

Bishop, c. 390–450
17 March

Ireland; Nigeria

I t is tempting to think that all must be Celtic mist and legend of the banishing snakes from Ireland variety where Patrick is concerned, but, in fact, we know a lot about what he was like through two documents written by him. The *Confessions* and the *Letter to Coroticus* provide a convincing self-portrait, which later wonder-laden, would-be devotional accounts only spoil.

He came from a prominent Christian family living near Carlisle, of which his father was an alderman, during the final decades of Roman rule in Britain. Shortly before he reached the age of 16, he was captured by raiders from northern Ireland and forced to herd sheep there for six years. This produced a deepening of his faith as he learned to cast himself on God's mercy. He wrote that he could feel the Spirit working within him.

He managed to escape and eventually found a ship that brought him to Wales or Cornwall, where the crew wandered aimlessly looking for food until Patrick assured them that God would provide, whereupon they came across wild pigs and then wild honey. Patrick found his way back to his family and at some stage was ordained priest. He visited Gaul and dreamed of going back to Ireland as a missionary. He was commissioned to do so by British 'seniors', who consecrated him bishop for the purpose.

For the rest of his life he evangelized Ireland, and his *Confessions* provide an account of his missions, though, like the Letters of St Paul,* they provide little information about where he actually went, apart from the fact that it was 'as far as the point where there is no beyond'. What they do show is his obvious love for his converts. Ireland had never been conquered by the Romans, and its people lived in small nomadic clans, worshipping many gods and goddesses, about whom Patrick could be scathing. He would have left the germs of small monastic communities as he went, thereby establishing the dominant pattern of church life in Ireland. The date and place of his death are not known, but what we know of his life fully justifies his title of 'Apostle to the Irish People'.

His traditional patronage of Ireland was officially confirmed in 1962. The previous year he had been named secondary (to the Virgin Mary*) patron of Nigeria.

Emblem: snakes, at his feet or being chased, from the legend that he drove them out of Ireland (in fact they never got there as Ireland separated from mainland Britain before they spread to its western parts)

St Brigid of Kildare

Abbess, c. 452–524
1 February

Ireland

Ireland's second patron was born about the time St Patrick*
died, but she is a far more mysterious and shadowy figure.
The root of her name, *Brig*, links her with the Druidic religion
dominant in Ireland before the coming of Christianity. Brig
was a goddess with many attributes, which were taken over and
applied to Brigid in the many fanciful Lives written about her
in later centuries.

The basic story underlying the legends connects her with
the monastery of Kildare, south-west of Dublin. It is reason-
ably conjectured that she consecrated herself to God as a virgin
at a young age and founded the monastery, going on to become
abbess. Kildare later became a double monastery, in which
monks generally laboured, while nuns – usually from a higher
social level – prayed, and the abbess had overall control. This
would have added to Brigid's prestige, even though Kildare
would not have been a double monastery in her day.

Brigid (after Brig) was responsible for life itself, for knowledge
and for fire. A sacred fire was kept burning at Kildare. The twenty
nuns each spent a night in turn to tend it, and after Brigid's death
the nineteenth nun put logs by the fire and said, 'Brigid, guard
your fire; this is your night.' In the morning the logs were burned
and the fire still alight. This comes from a twelfth-century
account, so the custom prevailed for many centuries.

Her legends make her live in different ages: she was said to have assisted Mary at Jesus' birth and was hailed as the Virgin Mary herself as a result of a priest's dream, becoming known as 'Mary of the Gael'. She even had her local version of the marriage feast at Cana, when she is said to have changed water into beer. She was also a patron of poets and metalworkers, and invoked for all kinds of healing. The stories all point to her wisdom and kindness to people and to animals. Rush crosses, known as 'Brigid's cross', are still made and hung in houses and barns to ward off disease and help with lambing. Irish pilgrims took her fame across Europe as far as Italy.

She was officially declared second patron of Ireland in the same decree that confirmed St Patrick* as principal patron, on 3 December 1962. Her feast-day, which is inherited from *Imbolg*, the first day of spring, was recently made a national holiday for women in Ireland.

St Benedict

Abbot and founder, c. 480–547
11 July (or 21 March)

Europe; farm workers; potholers; engineers and architects

The *Rule of St Benedict* is the foundational document for all monks in the Western world and has become a guide for lay people and even an inspiration of good business practice. Yet Benedict (which means simply 'blessed man') tells us nothing about himself in the Rule, and there is no account of his life until some 50 years after his death, when Pope St Gregory the Great included a short account, supposedly taken from several abbots who had known him, in his *Dialogues*.

Benedict was born in Nursia, near Rome, and sent to study in a Rome that had suffered from barbarian attacks and which he found so immoral that he escaped, first joining a group of committed Christians in a village and then becoming a hermit. He spent three years living in a cave, but he attracted the admiration of some local monks, who asked him to become their abbot. They did not like the life he proposed for them, and tried to poison him. After another attempt to found a community had made the parish priest jealous, he moved away, south to Monte Cassino.

He was by then about 45 years old. He collected monks around him and worked on the final version of the Rule. This drew on earlier works, using the best parts of several Rules and then improving on them, producing a sensible, practical, yet spiritually demanding guide to life. It insisted on obedience to the abbot (but obedience in love, not fear) and stability in the sense of lifelong belonging to one community. At a time when the Roman empire in the West was falling apart, it promised order and security by putting the greater good of a community before personal ambition.

Benedict was buried at Monte Cassino next to his sister, St Scholastica, and their tomb survived even the destruction of the monastery by Allied bombardment in World War II.

His patronage of Europe was declared by Pope Paul in 1964, when Monte Cassino had been rebuilt and was reconsecrated: Benedictine monks, the pope said, had provided the spiritual foundation of Europe. That of farm workers reflects the fact that his monks cultivated land when no one else was doing so; of potholers because he lived in a cave for three years; of engineers and architects because of his construction of Monte Cassino and ultimate responsibility for all the great monastic buildings: this was declared in 1957.

St David

Bishop, c. 520–89
1 March

Wales

David had to wait even longer than Benedict* – some 500 years – for an account of his life to be written, which must throw doubt on any facts, but this has not prevented him from being a much-loved patron saint of Wales. The 'biography' claims to draw on older accounts, and he is mentioned in earlier lists of saints, but it is really an attempt to make the see of St David's in Pembrokeshire as important as possible.

He was the son of a prince whose name means 'saint', was ordained priest, and after many travels settled with a community at Mynyw (Menevia). They followed an earlier and stricter Rule than Benedict's, eating only bread and vegetables, including the leeks that grew locally, and drinking only water from the local river. They ploughed the fields, without using oxen, and prayed, in community or mentally, continually.

David gained a great reputation as a preacher. The teaching of the Briton Pelagius – basically that human beings could ensure their own salvation without the help of divine grace – had been condemned as heresy by numerous councils in the fifth and sixth centuries, but still lingered on in Gaul and Britain. David attacked it with such zeal that he was proclaimed head of the Church in Wales by popular acclaim, and the legend developed that, when he was speaking at a local synod, the earth had risen up to form a hill, from which he could more easily be heard, while the Holy Spirit settled on his shoulder in the form of a white dove.

His patronage of Wales is traditional. By the late Middle Ages his feast was celebrated in Canterbury. Pilgrims from South Wales venerated his supposed remains at Glastonbury, but his shrine has always been at St David's.

Emblem: a white dove over a mound, from the above legend

St Columba of Iona

Abbot, c. 521–97

9 June

Ireland

The third patron saint of Ireland was a towering figure – physically, according to early accounts, as well as intellectually. Born of royal parentage in Ireland (where he is known as *Columcille*, a name made up of 'Columba' and 'cell', according to Bede), he was ordained priest in the north and established his first monastery in a fort in Derry (or Londonderry).

He preached around Ireland for fifteen years, making use of a voice that was said to carry for a mile, and founded many more monasteries. A dispute arising from an accidental death in a hurling match led to a war between his clan and the followers of King Diarmid. Three thousand died, and Columba was held responsible, narrowly escaping excommunication. He sailed for Scotland in 561, either to escape feelings of guilt or in response to an invitation from the king in the south and west, who was a relative.

He and his companions landed on a small island off Mull and set about building a monastery, which, as Iona, became the powerhouse of the Celtic Church. From there he set out to convert the Picts, over the mountains to the east – no easy task on account of their Druidic religion and the difficult terrain. He made several return visits to Ireland, but Iona was the centre of his activities for the rest of his life.

Books occupied an increasingly important part in his life.

He had earlier been rebuked for making a copy of Jerome's*
Psalter, which he had borrowed from Finnian of Moville, but
there were no 'copyright' problems over copying the Gospels,
and he is reputed to have made over 300 copies. Before he died
he blessed Iona, prophesying that it would be honoured in Ireland, by 'even barbarous and foreign nations', and by 'saints of
other churches', as indeed has proved to be the case. Bede
praised its monks for their 'purity of life, their love of God,
and their loyalty to the monastic Rule'.

His patronage of Ireland was confirmed by the same 1962
decree that gave the title to Patrick* and Brigid.*

Emblems: wild beasts, from his love of them portrayed in the
Life by his successor Adomnán; sunbeams over his head, for
the power of his preaching

St Eligius

Bishop, c. 588–660
1 December

Goldsmiths, silversmiths, jewellers, metalworkers, coin and medal collectors; horses and veterinarians; blacksmiths; motor mechanics

E ligius is one of many bishops from the period in the history of Gaul known as Merovingian (from about AD 500 to 750) to have been declared saints. He is also a saint whose patronages derive (mainly) from his life, as he was a prodigiously talented metalworker by trade: several of his pieces survive to this day.

He spent much of his life as a layman carrying out his trade, and it was this that brought him to the notice of kings of the Franks. King Clotaire II gave him materials to make a state chair, and by skilful design Eligius made the gold and precious stones stretch to two chairs, for which he was rewarded with the post of master of the mint in Marseilles. He became a trusted adviser to the next king, Dagobert I, and it was during this period that he was commissioned to make magnificent reliquaries for St Martin* at Tours, SS Denys and Genevieve at Paris, and several others.

He became a wealthy man, but was generous to the poor, who crowded around his house. He befriended a younger man, Audoenus, who was later credited with writing his Life, though this is now thought to be a later work. Both men felt strongly drawn to the monastic life; the king would not let them leave his court, but encouraged them to found monasteries. In around 641, both were chosen as bishops, Eligius of Noyon and Tournai and Audoenus archbishop of Rouen, and they were consecrated together at Noyon.

Eligius proved an outstanding bishop, a fine preacher and a brave missionary. In the neighbouring Low Countries he was reviled as foreign and 'Roman', but he persevered and made many converts. With the queen-regent, St Bathild (who had been sold into slavery as a child), he enacted church laws to improve the treatment of slaves and for many years personally ransomed many, some of whom joined him in his workshop. He died from a fever and soon became one of the most popular French saints, called Saint Eloi there and known to Chaucer as 'Saint Loy'.

His patronage of goldsmiths and similar workers is obvious and traditional. Coins struck by him survive, and he was formally recognized as patron of the Argentinian Society of Coin Collectors in 1983. That of horses and those who treat them derives from a legend that his horse was stolen by a bishop shortly after his death, took sick, and refused to recover until restored to its rightful owner, a priest to whom he had left it. This has been extended to blacksmiths, who make the shoes to keep horses on the road, and then to those who work in garages (or gas stations) as motor vehicles have taken over the role of horses as means of transport.

Emblems: reflect both traditions of patronage and include a hammer, chalice, anvil, crown, shrine, horseshoe and horse's leg

SS Cyril and Methodius

Missionaries, bishop, 827–69 and 815–84
14 February

Europe; Yugoslavia; Czech Republic; ecumenism; converts

The brothers Cyril and Methodius (who was the elder but is listed second as their joint feast-day is now – in the West – on the day of Cyril's death) were missionaries to the parts of central Europe now occupied by the provinces of Bohemia and Moravia, which make up the Czech Republic, and further east: modern Serbia, Slovenia and Croatia. Ethnic and other quarrels in the region were as bad in their day as they have been in ours.

They were sent to Moravia by the eastern emperor in response to a request for missionaries from Duke Ratislav, who stipulated that they must speak Slavonic, which the brothers had done from childhood. Slavonic was at the time a spoken language only, and in order to provide liturgical texts they had to devise an alphabet. Using Greek with some additional characters, they produced what is now the Cyrillic script still used by Russian and other Slav languages. They translated parts of the Bible and Greek and Roman liturgical texts, and effectively became the fathers of Slavonic literature.

They made many converts in Moravia, but were opposed by the bishop of Passau, who wanted to extend the influence of the Bavarian Church eastward. They appealed to the patriarch of Constantinople, but ended up in Rome (because Cyril had supposed relics of St Clement, miraculously rescued from the

Black Sea, where he was said to have been drowned with an anchor round his neck ...), where Cyril died and Pope Hadrian II backed their liturgical reforms.

Methodius returned to his missions and was consecrated archbishop of Sirmium (near Belgrade), which made him head of the eastern part of the Western (owing allegiance to Rome, not Constantinople) Church. He was arrested and imprisoned by the Bavarian authorities, then released on the orders of the pope, while his liturgy was banned for ten years. He spent his final years working on his translation of the Bible.

Their patronage of (the former) Yugoslavia dates from 1914; of (the former) Czechoslovakia from 1914, and of Bohemia and Moravia separately from 1935 and 1936. Pope John Paul II declared them patrons of Europe (with St Benedict*) in 1980, to proclaim the unity of Eastern and Western Europe, which makes them also (undeclared) patrons of ecumenism.

St Wenceslas

Martyr, c. 907–29
28 September

Czech Republic and Slovakia; brewers

Wenceslas was proclaimed duke of Bohemia in 922, some 60 years after the mission of SS Cyril and Methodius,* and was educated in Latin and Slavonic by his grandmother, who is venerated as St Ludmilla. The Bavarians were still trying to gain influence over the relatively new Slav Church; while paganism was not entirely extinct, forming a faction supported by Wenceslas' own mother, Drahomíra.

His father was killed in battle in 921, plunging the dukedom into violent conflict. Drahomíra's supporters murdered Ludmilla, for which she was banished. Wenceslas brought Ludmilla's body to Prague and recalled Drahomíra from banishment, after which she no longer opposed him. The main threat now came from his brother Boleslas, who had a power base in the east of the country.

Wenceslas, still only 15 at the start of his rule, set about curbing the power of the nobles, improving education and supporting the spread of Christianity. He also married and had a son, thus removing Boleslas from being his successor. But he angered the nationalist faction by accepting the (German) emperor Henry I as his overlord, and Boleslas became their leader. He tricked his brother into attending the nominal dedication of a new church, where he and his nobles set upon Wenceslas and murdered him.

Although he had died for political rather than purely religious motives, he was immediately honoured as a martyr. His body was eventually enshrined in St Vitus' Church in Prague, and the stories told of him depicted him as the ideal Christian prince – and nothing to do with the 'good King Wenceslas' of the carol.

He was named patron of Czechoslovakia, then of Bohemia and Moravia, in the same decrees as SS Cyril and Methodius. His patronage of brewers reflects Czech excellence in the brewing of beer (as more and more tourists who sample Pilsner Urquell and the original Budweiser in their homeland will testify), rather than any association with his life.

Second Millennium

St Margaret of Scotland

Queen, c. 1045–93
16 November

Scotland

Margaret was a granddaughter of Edmund Ironside, king of Wessex, who had fled to Hungary with his family to escape Danish invaders of England. Her father was Edmund's son Edward the Atheling, and Margaret was born in Hungary and educated there.

In 1057 King Edward the Confessor summoned her father back to make him heir to the throne of England, but he died soon after his return. Disputes over the succession broke out, and Margaret took refuge in Scotland. She was welcomed by King Malcolm III, and married him in 1070. They lived happily until his death, with six sons and two daughters born to the marriage.

The manners of the Scottish court were somewhat rough, and she introduced more civilized continental ways. She was also devoted to the advancement of the Church, and she revived St Columba's* decayed monastery of Iona, as well as developing the priory of Dunfermline, which Malcolm had founded and which became the royal burial place. She cared for her husband, her children and the poor. Malcolm never learned to read, but appreciated her learning and talents, especially for needlework.

In November 1093 Malcolm was killed fighting King William II of England at the battle of Alnwick in Northumberland.

Margaret was already terminally ill and died after accepting his death as the will of God. His body was brought back to Dunfermline, and she was buried beside him after her death on 16 November.

Shortly after her death, someone who knew her well wrote an account of her life and holiness, and although this follows a conventional pattern, her character shows through. She soon had a popular local cult, but it was not until 1250 that Pope Innocent IV officially declared her a saint. When the English sacked Dunfermline in 1560, her body and Malcolm's were taken to El Escorial, Philip II's monastery-palace near Madrid. Her head had been separated to allow more widespread veneration, and was taken first to Edinburgh and then to the English College at Douai in northern France.

Her patronage of Scotland was officially confirmed in 1673.

Emblems: a Greek cross and silver saltire

St Bernard

Abbot and Doctor, 1090–1153

20 August

Gibraltar; beekeepers

As a young man, Bernard led 30 noblemen to the abbey of Cîteaux to join the new Cistercian Order. He came to dominate the twelfth century: as a churchman and statesman, preaching devotion to Mary and the Crusades, and as an inexhaustible and brilliant letter-writer, he made his influence felt throughout Europe, effectively controlling the actions of kings and popes.

He was one of seven children (all but two subsequently canonized or beatified) born into an aristocratic family from Burgundy. He decided he would be 'a knight of Christ', and most of those he led to Cîteaux were his friends and relatives. Three years later the abbot, St Stephen Harding, asked him to found another monastery at Clairvaux. As abbot, he made this the chief focus of Cistercian expansion, with 24 new monasteries founded from it.

It often took several secretaries taking simultaneous dictation to keep up with his output of letters. From deciding all aspects of ethics, discipline, architecture and art in his monasteries he moved on to the wider European stage, advising popes, kings and anyone who applied to him. He settled disputes over succession to bishoprics, established a Rule for the Templars, railed ruthlessly against anyone whose views smacked to him of heresy, especially poor Peter Abelard, and, even more ferociously (though unsuccessfully), the Albigensians of southern France. One of his pupils became pope as Eugenius III in 1145 and asked Bernard to preach the Second Crusade. This was a disaster, for which Bernard was widely, if unfairly, blamed.

His journeys became triumphal tours, as he acquired a huge reputation as a healer, and he often had to be protected from over-enthusiastic crowds. He was also a deep contemplative and a major theologian, promulgating devotion to Mary and above all love of Christ: 'love in action' might stand as his motto. After settling a last major dispute, he died at Clairvaux on 20 August 1153. He was canonized 21 years later and formally declared a Doctor of the Church in 1830.

He was declared patron of Gibraltar in 1914, though there is no obvious connection with his life; he is also patron of beekeepers, as he was called the 'honey-tongued' doctor.

Emblems: beehive, for 'honey-tongued'; white dog, for the white Cistercian habit

St Hildegard of Bingen

Abbess, 1098–179
17 September

Philologists; Esperantists

O ne of the most accomplished and extraordinary women of any age, Hildegard began seeing visions and hearing voices at the age of three. She was sent by her German nobleman father to be educated by an 'anchoress' named Jutta, who formed her pupils into a religious community. Hildegard succeeded her as abbess in 1136.

Her confessor encouraged her to record her 'revelations', and the result, dictated over years, formed a three-volume work known as *Scivias* (a shortened form of the Latin for 'Know the ways of the Lord'). This was approved by the archbishop of Mainz as being 'from God' and then shown to the pope, who had it examined by a theological commission, which also cleared it.

One of her visions was of a place on a hill, which she identified as the Rupertsberg, near Bingen on the Rhine, and after some struggle she moved her community there. She wrote music and hymns for her nuns, devised an early form of Esperanto, cultivated herbs, and composed books on natural history and medicine – in which she described the circulation of the blood, five centuries before Harvey. She also illustrated *Scivias*, in a decorative style that foreshadows William Blake, and produced two further accounts of her visions.

She was afraid of no one and despatched letters to everyone from the pope to kings and downward: advising, warning, rebuking. When she allowed the body of a young man who had once been excommunicated to be buried in the convent grounds, the bishop forbade the nuns to celebrate the liturgy. Hildegard told him: 'Those ... who ... impose silence on churches in which singing in God's honour can be heard will not deserve to hear the glorious choir of angels that praises God in heaven.' The bishop relented.

She has become an inspiration for Christian feminists and for the 'deep ecology' movement. Her music has been revived, recorded on CDs (one with her description of herself, a 'feather on the breath of God', as its title) and become very popular. She was never formally canonized, though her cult was approved in 1324, and she now has the title 'saint' in the new Roman Martyrology.

As she has never formally been declared a saint, her patronages of philologists, on account of her learning, and of Esperantists, for her early experiments with such a language, are popular or traditional.

St Francis of Assisi

Founder, 1182–226
4 October

Italy; Italian merchants; ecology and ecologists

B orn the son of a wealthy cloth merchant trading in Florence, Francis joined the town's army when he was 20, and
was taken prisoner in an unsuccessful war against Assisi's larger
neighbour, Perugia. Released after a year, he set off to join the
papal forces in Rome, but he was turned back by a dream,
which he interpreted as a call to help the poor and sick.

Praying in the church of San Damiano one day, he heard a
voice telling him to repair the church, which was in ruins. He
sold some of his father's cloth to pay for the repairs, and his
father took him to the bishop's court, where he renounced his
inheritance by stripping off his fine clothes. Dressed from then
on only in a workman's smock, he took the Gospel counsel of
poverty quite literally and began preaching repentance in Assisi.

Others soon felt called to join him; he called them 'lesser
brothers' and devised a communal way of life, never expecting
that this would have to apply to large numbers; but it soon did, so
he organized them into provinces. After a young woman named
Clare* asked to join, a 'Second Order' for enclosed nuns was started at San Damiano, followed by a Third, for lay supporters.

Francis set his heart on converting the Muslims, and though
he failed in this, he gave his followers a permanent missionary
calling, which soon took them as far as China and, centuries
later, to the New World. He also, after a tussle in his mind

between 'lady poverty' and 'lady learning', approved Franciscan theological schools at the new universities.

He retired in 1220 to live a hermit's life, and it is to this period that the famous stories of taming a wolf and preaching to the birds belong. He also bore the marks of Christ's passion – the *stigmata* – with painful, visible wounds in his hands and feet that hurt and bled: the first saint in history of whom this phenomenon is recorded. His last years were clouded by sickness, and he died outside Assisi after paying a last visit to Clare, which inspired his 'Canticle of Brother Sun'. He had brought a Church generally seen as corrupt and wealthy back to a spirituality based firmly on the Gospel message, which has been heard – by some, at least – ever since.

He has been traditional patron of Italy since shortly after his death; this was officially confirmed in 1939. As he had been a merchant, he is patron of Italian merchants, confirmed in 1952. Pope John Paul II declared him patron of ecology and ecologists in 1979, citing his references to 'Brother Sun' and 'Sister Moon'.

Emblems: stigmata; lily; lamb

St Antony of Padua

Franciscan friar, 1195–231
13 June

Portugal; lost articles; the poor; harvests

Antony was born in Portugal and became an Augustinian friar, spending eight years at Coïmbra, where he studied the Bible and meditated. When the first Franciscan missionaries were killed in Morocco, and their relics were brought to Portugal, Antony was inspired to become a missionary and a martyr like them. However, the Augustinians were not a missionary Order, so he left them and joined the Franciscans.

He sailed for Morocco to convert the Moors, but was soon sent home when he became seriously ill. A storm landed his ship in Sicily instead of in Portugal. There he was told that the Franciscans were about to hold a general chapter in Assisi, so he set off and there met Francis,* who despatched him to a hermitage to carry out menial tasks and pray. He seems not to have revealed his deep biblical learning, perhaps because of language barriers, perhaps because the early Franciscans were still not very interested in learning.

When a joint ordination service for both Franciscans and Dominicans was held at Forli, it was discovered that neither Order had appointed a preacher: the latter expecting their Franciscan hosts to do so, the former expecting this of the 'Order of Preachers'. Antony was asked to preach, and delivered 'a flood of divine eloquence', as a result of which he was asked to preach all over Lombardy, where he drew crowds of thousands and inspired many to repent.

Francis, then coming to terms with learning, appointed him the Order's first reader in theology, which he taught at Bologna. He was then sent to convert the Albigensians in southern France and preached against them so vehemently that he was called 'the hammer of the heretics'. Hammering them, however, was possibly not the best way to win their hearts and minds, as St Dominic was to realize a little later. Antony was recalled to Italy when Francis died in 1226, and spent his last few years preaching around Padua. His health was fragile, and he died at the early age of 36, upon which he was immediately hailed as a saint. He was canonized the following year, and over the centuries legends grew around him and he became one of the most popular saints in the calendar.

Invocation of him to find lost articles – 'St Antony, St Antony, where art thou?' – seems to have developed from the generally miraculous tone of his legends rather than from any specific incident; many traditional Catholic households will swear to its efficacy. Devotion to him in his native land remained strong, and he was formally declared patron of Portugal, with St Francis Borgia,* in 1934. Miracles attributed to him include preserving a harvest from devastation by a flock of birds and restoring a cornfield trampled by a crowd listening to him preach. These led to the baking of 'St Antony's bread' on his feast-day, which was distributed to the poor: hence his patronage of them and of harvests.

Emblems: lily and book, for purity and learning; preaching to fishes; holding the infant Jesus (legendary); vanquishing the devil (also legendary)

St Clare of Assisi

Founder, c. 1193–253

11 August

Embroiderers; television

Daughter of a prominent family of Assisi, Clare annoyed her male relatives by refusing to marry, which meant they could not marry off her younger sisters either. Hearing Francis* preach sealed this refusal permanently: she went to the Portiuncula, just outside the city, where the first Franciscans were living, and took a vow to become a nun. The offended males broke into the convent in which she was lodged and tried to drag her out of the church. Clinging to the altar cloths, she showed them her shorn hair and persuaded them to leave her as a bride of Christ.

Francis installed her in another house at San Damiano, just outside Assisi, and her widowed mother, her sisters and several other women from aristocratic families came to join the new community, of which Clare became abbess. They lived according to a basic Rule drawn up by Francis, with Clare insisting that their first duty was to poverty, which meant that they had to be able to go outside the convent to beg, while church officials went on trying to force them to accept complete enclosure, financed by rents. In the end, she wrote her own Rule, the first woman founder to do so, forbidding the ownership of property, either as individuals or as a community.

Clare's Rule imposed an austere way of life on her nuns, but she adopted even more severe austerity herself, often fasting until she became ill, forcing her to modify her practices. She remained as abbess for 40 years, and her combination of poverty with some freedom of movement was soon being copied by other convents, inside and outside Italy. Clare acted as servant to all, while remaining resolutely in control. It is said that when the Saracens attacked Assisi, she exposed the Blessed Sacrament on the walls, which made the 'infidel' army withdraw. Her fame of holiness was such that Pope Innocent II visited her twice toward the end of her life, saying that he wished he were in as little need of absolution as she.

She was canonized just two years after her death.

She is traditional patron of embroiderers, as she spent her times of illness embroidering vestments. She is said to have seen the crib and heard singing one Christmas when confined to her bed, just as if she had been in church, and this inspired Pope Pius XII to proclaim her patron of television in 1958.

Emblems: lilies in her hand or on her head, for purity; holding a monstrance or trampling on a scimitar, from the legend of stopping the Saracen army

St Bridget

Founder, 1303–73
23 July

Sweden

B ridget was married for 28 years and had eight children. When she was about 32 years old she was made lady-in-waiting to the new queen of Sweden, Blanche of Namur. She and her husband made a pilgrimage to Santiago de Compostela in 1340, in mourning for the death of their youngest son, and her husband died soon after their return.

The outward events of her life were dictated – quite literally, she believed – by Christ, who spoke to her frequently and in great detail in a series of visions, the content of which she told her confessors, who wrote them down. They included graphic accounts of his nativity and crucifixion, differing from the New Testament stories in some respects, and went on to provide a full Rule for a new religious foundation she was told to make: the Order of the Most Holy Saviour, known as the Brigettines.

This was the time of rival claims to the papacy and the flight of popes from Rome to Avignon. Bridget's revelations led her to castigate Pope Clement VI in the harshest possible terms, but even if he believed her words came directly from Christ, he was not moved. She delivered 'His' warnings to the kings of England and France, enjoining them to desist from the Hundred Years War, again with no effect, and to King

Magnus of Sweden, who was engaged in grabbing the land of pagan neighbours, but he to failed to relent.

Disillusioned, Bridget left Sweden and went to Rome. She was given a house there and dictated another long series of revelations on the association of the Virgin Mary with God's mercy and justice. Pope Urban V returned temporarily to Rome in 1367 – she warned him he would soon die if he returned to Avignon – he did so and died four months later. She prophesied doom to the people of Rome for their dissolute ways, which made her unpopular and caused her to be turned out of her house.

She set out on pilgrimage to the Holy Land with her daughter Catherine (also a saint) and two sons. She persevered through a shipwreck and the death of one son, and in the Holy Land she had detailed visions of events in Jesus' life in the actual places where they were supposed to have taken place. She was ill by the time she returned, and died in Rome in July 1373. Her remains were taken in triumph to her first foundation in Sweden.

She was canonized in 1391, ostensibly for the piety of her life and her works of charity, as the Church is always careful not to

endorse 'private revelations'. Hers, however, soon translated into several languages, had a long-lasting effect on the devotional life of Christians. The Brigetttine Order still has some 30 houses, spread over Europe, the USA and India.

She was recognized as patron of Sweden in 1891 by Pope Leo XIII, and this was confirmed in 1926.

St Catherine of Siena

Doctor, 1347–80
29 April

Italy; Italian nuns; Italian nurses; women in Catholic Action

L ike St Bridget,* Catherine was a visionary who admon-
ished the popes at Avignon; unlike Bridget, she refused to
marry and made herself as unattractive as possible to discour-
age suitors.

She was born, one of twins, into a wealthy and very numerous family – there were already 22 children. She was as strong-
willed as she was devout, and used fasting to control her will
and to attempt to control others. Had she lived today, she
would almost certainly be diagnosed as anorexic. She ate virtually nothing from the age of 21 to her death at 33, combining
this with a life of sustained activity.

From an early age she experienced 'mystical espousal' to
Christ, but the message she received from him was that she
could not keep him to herself but had to make her love for him
work in practical ways. She combined membership of a devout
sisterhood with action on behalf of the sick and the poor.
Then she felt Christ call her to preach and, with the help of
her confessor and later biographer, Raymund of Capua, who
reminded her that Jesus had chosen the weak and humble to
spread his message, she overcame her cultural resistance to the
idea of a woman preaching.

Once convinced that she was inspired by the Holy Spirit,
Catherine preached in no uncertain fashion: she attacked the

social scourge of poverty and inveighed against corruption in the Church. She also sent letters to all from Pope Gregory XI down: she treated him like an errant boy, '*telling*' him to get back from Avignon ... She went there, but other forces proved stronger than she for the time being. Gregory did return, but died before resolving the quarrels. She then moved to Rome to support his successor, Urban VI, against Clement VII, an 'antipope' elected by a rival faction, thus starting the Great Schism.

She lived in Rome in a 'spiritual family' she gathered around her, whom she instructed through dictating what she called 'my book', known as *The Dialogue*, which recorded her mystical experiences and her views on the Church. It was this masterly work, astonishing for someone with so little education, that was to earn her the title of Doctor of the Church in 1970: the only lay person, let alone woman, to be so designated. A complete hunger strike to make herself a sacrifice on behalf of the

Church finally ruined her precarious health. Raymund completed his biography of her in 1395, but ongoing divisions in the Church delayed her canonization for over 60 years.

She was declared patron of women involved in Catholic Action by Pope St Pius X; in 1939 Pius XII made her a principal patron of Italy, with St Francis of Assisi,* for her efforts to bring the papacy back to Rome; and in 1944 the same pope made her patron of Italian nurses, for her practical work with the sick.

Emblems: crown of thorns; crucifix; cross and heart; wedding ring; lily; dove

St Joan of Arc

1412–31
30 May

France; French soldiers

Y et another visionary with an implacable will, Joan pres-
ents a number of problems, with queries over her identi-
ty, the source of her 'voices', the nature of her holiness and the
cause for which she died. Her heroism and patriotism, however,
are beyond doubt.

A peasant girl from the Meuse region of eastern France, she
had a normal happy childhood until, at the age of 14, she
began to 'hear voices' calling her to save France. It needed
saving from the English, who claimed its throne and controlled
most of the north and much of the south-west, and from
internal strife between the house of Orléans and the dukes of
Burgundy, who sided with the English. Joan saw her mission as
enabling the dauphin, the elder son of Charles VI, to be
crowned at the traditional site of Reims, then in English
hands.

Despite ridicule and opposition, she saw the dauphin and
was given troops to lead into battle. A panel summoned to
investigate her religious orthodoxy could find no fault with her.
Her forces then took Orléans from the English, inflicted a
crushing defeat on them at Patay, and induced them to surren-
der Troyes, the gateway north to Reims. She persuaded the
reluctant and frivolous dauphin to go to Reims, and stood
beside him at his coronation on 7 July 1429. She had, amazingly,

accomplished her mission, but she decided to go on campaigning. She was wounded outside Paris, and then in spring 1430 was captured by the Burgundians when trying to relieve the siege of Compiègne.

The English persuaded the duke of Burgundy to hand her over to them, planning to take revenge by trying her for witchcraft. A tribunal headed by the ambitious bishop of Beauvais, Cauchon, had effectively decided the verdict in advance. Joan defended herself valiantly, asserting her loyalty to her voices, to the Church and to God, but she was condemned as a 'relapsed heretic', handed over to the secular authorities, and sentenced to be burned at the stake. This took place in Rouen on the following morning, 30 May 1431. One of the witnesses, a secretary of the English king Henry VI, had the prescience to remark: 'We are lost. We have burned a saint.'

She was rehabilitated by the Church in 1456, after a tribunal summoned by the pope in response to pressure from her family. It was not until the twentieth century, however, that she was beatified, in 1910, and then canonized, in 1920. The Church

has never called her a martyr, implying that she died in defence of France rather than of the Faith. Two of the saints who inspired her were in 1969 declared not to have existed, but for most Catholics, many Protestants (who see her as combating a corrupt Church), French and other nationalists, and feminists, she is an ongoing example of integrity.

She was declared 'secondary' patron of France (the Virgin Mary* being the principal one) in 1922 and confirmed in 1962. Her patronage of French soldiers was proclaimed in 1952.

St Frances of Rome

Founder, 1384–440
9 March

Widows; motorists

B orn to wealthy and devout parents in the Trastevere ('across the Tiber') district of Rome, Frances wanted a religious life for herself, but her parents had arranged a marriage to a young man named Lorenzo Poziano. The wedding took place when she was 13, a normal age at the time. Her husband treated her with love and respect, but she was not happy, and with her sister-in-law Vanozza, began to plan how to reconcile a religious life with a married one.

They visited the sick, distributed alms and set up an oratory in the family palace. In 1400 Frances gave birth to her first son, and the following year found herself head of the household. When war brought famine and disaster to Rome, Frances had soon given virtually all the family supplies to the poor and went out begging for more. In 1408, by which time she had given birth to a second son, her elder boy was seized as a hostage, but he was given back when the horse on which his captors placed him refused to budge. Lorenzo was stabbed, and she gradually nursed him back to health, but then he and the elder son were taken once more and exiled.

She and Vanozza opened a hospital for plague victims in the ruins of the family palace. Fame of her powers of healing soon spread all over Rome. She attributed them to a guardian angel, whom she could constantly see. Lorenzo returned from exile in broken health, and Frances cared for him while developing a group of like-minded women into a religious community. They did not take vows, but lived in common, devoting their lives to works of charity. Frances entered the community when Lorenzo died, and was compelled to become superior. She died on 9 March 1440. Her last words were: 'The angel has finished his work.'

She is the traditional patron of widows on account of the course of her life. In 1925 she was made patron of motorists, especially of Roman motorists, perhaps because the light from her angel enabled her to see in the dark. (Anyone who knows Rome might think its pedestrians more in need of her protection.)

Emblem: an angel

Fra Angelico

Dominican friar, c. 1400–55
18 February

Christian artists

T he painter known to the world as Fra Angelico, the 'angelic brother', is the exception in the present work in that he is not (yet) a canonized saint, though he has finally been beatified (in 1982) as Blessed John of Fiesole.

He was born near Florence into the di Piero family and christened Guido. By 1417 he was a member of a painting fraternity, and he joined the Dominicans in 1420, so spending his adult life as a Dominican friar. He became the disciple of a monk-painter known as Lorenzo Monaco. His community moved from Fiesole into the convent of San Marco in Florence, where the ruling Florentine family and great patrons of the arts, the Medicis, sponsored a major course of enlargement, giving Brother John the opportunity to decorate the walls with a unique series of murals.

These were intended as aids to devotion, not as decoration. His claim to sanctity lies in his sacramental approach to his work. He was, as Ruskin remarked many centuries later, an 'inspired saint' rather than 'an artist, properly so called'. He painted a sacred scene in each of the friar's cells and at the end of each corridor. His work bridges the Middle Ages and the Renaissance, combining the devotion of the former with the new understanding of perspective and the humanism of the latter. The scenes are natural, gentle and inviting. Often, the inclusion of the figure of a friar brings home the message that they are intended as a personal reminder of the Dominican calling to preach the gospel truths conveyed in the subject matter.

His work at San Marco spread his fame to Rome and elsewhere, and he was called to execute other commissions, including two chapels in the Vatican as well as work in St Peter's and in the pope's private study. These last prevented him from completing a great Last Judgement fresco in Orvieto Cathedral.

He was not just a painter in religious life but played an active part in the affairs of the Order and the Church, so that at one stage he was proposed as archbishop of Florence. He preferred to remain as prior of Fiesole and suggested his friend Antoninus, who proved one of the great archbishops and became a saint and patron of Florence.

He was declared patron of Christian artists by Pope John Paul II in 1982, at his beatification ceremony.

St John of God

Founder, 1495–550
8 March

Booksellers and all engaged in the book trade; hospitals, the sick and nurses

John might be called a *conquistador* of the rights of the poor, rather than of other lands. His childhood was strange and adventurous. Apparently abducted from his village in Portugal by a priest, who left him in a Spanish border town, he was taken in and educated there, joined the army, escaped after a false accusation of theft threatened his life, and fought the Turks in Hungary. Finding his way back to his village, he found that his mother had died of grief and his father had become a Dominican. He resolved to work only for God and tried for a time to free Christians enslaved by Muslims in North Africa.

Forced to return to Spain, he made a living as an itinerant seller of religious books and pictures. Arriving in Granada, he heard St John of Avila preach, which threw him into a veritable frenzy of repentance. He ran around the streets shrieking and tearing his hair and was incarcerated in the lunatic asylum. Months of flogging and solitary confinement (the accepted treatment) had no effect; then John of Avila visited him and told him to stop repenting and do something worthwhile. He calmed down, but stayed to minister to other inmates, besides attending the sick in hospitals.

The Virgin of Guadalupe (at her original shrine in Extremadura, not the later, more famous, one in Mexico) showed him his mission by holding out clothing, meaning, he realized, that he was to clothe the child Jesus. Back in Granada, he somehow acquired an empty house and 46 beds and mattresses, and was soon running a full and highly efficient hospital. Sleeping only one hour a night, he nursed and begged; his standards of hygiene were remarkable, as was his care for his patients' spiritual welfare. When the inhabitants told him he could not support the hospital by begging, they found themselves contributing supplies and services on a scale that enabled him to found a bigger hospital. When this became too small, the archbishop gave him a deserted monastery.

He still worked and begged ceaselessly. He was received by the king and showered with gifts – which he immediately gave to the poor. His health finally succumbed to a crazy attempt to collect firewood from the River Genil in spate. When he died on his 55th birthday, all Granada turned out for his funeral. His helpers were established as the Brothers of St John of God in 1586.

His patronages stem obviously from his life; that of the book trade is traditional, while that of hospitals and the sick was confirmed in 1886, and extended to nurses in 1930.

St Ignatius Loyola

Founder, 1491–556
31 July

Retreats and spiritual exercises; invoked against scruples

I gnatius spent his youth as a page to the court treasurer of King Ferdinand of Spain, which taught him to gamble, womanize, quarrel, duel and read romances of chivalry. This life came to an end when Charles V succeeded Ferdinand and removed the treasurer from office. Ignatius joined the army of the viceroy of Navarre, serving for five years. His military career also came to an end when the French besieged Pamplona and a cannonball broke one of his legs and damaged the other. The French reset his leg, but he limped for the rest of his life.

He asked for novels of chivalry to read while convalescing, but was given *The Golden Legend* and forced to read about saints instead of knights errant. These inspired him with the idea of being a 'knight for Christ', and he set out to do penance by a pilgrimage to the Holy Land. He stopped at the monastery of Montserrat near Barcelona, made a general confession, and began to plan his great literary and spiritual legacy, the *Spiritual Exercises*. Ten months later he went on to Jerusalem, then returned to study, first at Barcelona, then at the two great Castilian universities of Alcalá and Salamanca. He gathered a group of disciples around him and began to wear clerical dress, which led the Inquisition to examine the *Spiritual Exercises*. These were pronounced orthodox, but he saw France as a more favourable climate and moved to Paris for six formative years.

Two further years of study in Venice led him to gather his companions there and form them into a 'Company of Jesus', run on military lines, commanded by God, and dedicated to mission and charitable work. They were ordained priests and wanted to set sail east to convert Muslims, but they could not find a ship and went to Rome instead. On the way, Ignatius had a vision that confirmed him in his course. The group offered their services to the pope and were soon in demand from other rulers. They were approved as the 'Society of Jesus' in 1540, and Ignatius spent the rest of his life directing their activities from Rome.

Just as the Mendicant Orders (Franciscans and Dominicans) had dominated the religious spirit of the Middle Ages, so the Jesuits (as members of the Society became known) set the

tone of the Catholic Counter-Reformation. Highly educated, trained in judgement by the *Spiritual Exercises*, individualistic though obedient to superiors, they spread rapidly through the Old and New Worlds, educating children and adults in a humanistic and modernizing spirit, and influencing literature, painting and theatre. (Jesuits appropriately provide the next two entries here.)

Ignatius' patronage of retreats and spiritual exercises, meaning those who give retreats and courses and those who attend them, was declared by Pope Pius XI in 1922. He is invoked by those suffering from scruples because the *Spiritual Exercises* provide guidance for such.

St Francis Xavier

Jesuit missionary, 1506–52
3 December

Outer Mongolia, India, Pakistan; foreign missions; tourism, Spanish tourists;
Argentinean pelota *players*

Though he died before Ignatius,* Francis was one of his first followers and so is placed after him here. Like Ignatius, he came from the Spanish Basque Country. He studied at the university of Paris, where he met Ignatius. In 1534 he was one of seven companions who vowed to live together in poverty and were later ordained in Venice.

He was one of the first to be appointed to a mission, in his case the East Indies, then ruled by Portugal, which meant that his departure was controlled by the Portuguese king, who valued his presence in Lisbon so highly that for some time he would not let him go. Eventually he sailed for Goa in April 1541, taking an Italian priest and a Portuguese ordinand, and arriving in May the following year.

The Portuguese, despite the nominal Christianity of their colonialism, ruled with scant regard for the Gospel. Francis did what he could to educate, help and evangelize the poorest of the native population, and after five months extended his mission to the low-caste Parava people of southern India. He wrote back to King John of Portugal, telling him that the violent and debauched behaviour of the colonists was an obstacle to conversion. Between 1545 and 1549 he seems to have worked in and around Indonesia, then, hearing of the closed country of Japan, he decided to go there, landing in August 1549.

He taught himself Japanese and produced a basic textbook of Christian doctrine in Japanese. A year later, having made a hundred converts, he and his companions moved to Miyako (now Kyoto), where the ruler gave them an empty Buddhist monastery. There were soon 2,000 converts, and the foundations for Japan's 'Christian century' (which was to end in brutal and large-scale martyrdoms) were laid. Francis left two Portuguese priests in charge, returned to India to put right abuses that had arisen during his absence, and then sailed east again to convert China.

This vast ambition was never realized. Disputes and sickness led to a miserable death on 3 December 1552. Even if not all his work in particular regions proved lasting, he set a new tone for 'foreign' missions, raising a prophetic voice against exploitation and injustice. He was canonized in 1622 (with Ignatius).

His patronage of missions derives from his life and was confirmed in 1904; that of Outer Mongolia was declared in 1914, of tourism in 1952, of India in 1962, and of Pakistan in 1971. He was reputed to have played the Basque ball game of *pelota* (the fastest in the world), and Pope Paul VI granted Argentinean players his special patronage in 1978.

St Thomas More

Descended from a legal family, More joined the household of John Morton, who was both archbishop of Canterbury and Lord Chancellor of England, at the age of 13. He went on to study at Oxford, from which his father removed him after two years, fearing that his love of the classics was harming his Catholic faith.

Studying in London did not lessen his love of the classics, which he shared and discussed with his friend Erasmus of Rotterdam, another scholar concerned to reconcile his faith with his humanist learning. More lived austerely at the London Charterhouse until he married. His wife, Jane Colt, died four years later, leaving him with four children. He married again, and with his second wife, Alice Middleton, established a household that was part monastery and part school, loving and hospitable as well as a centre of learning and prayer. He took equal care over the education of his daughters as he did his son.

His continued studies and practice in law brought him a flourishing career. With a learned and energetic new king, Henry VIII, coming to the throne in 1510, he was knighted, made Speaker of the House of Commons and given other public offices. In 1515 Henry's Chancellor, Cardinal Wolsey, sent him on a delegation to the Netherlands, where an unexpected stay of six months gave him some leisure for the first time in many years. He spent this writing most of *Utopia* (meaning 'no place'), a playful but learned description of an ideal State, somewhat resembling Plato's *Republic*. Back in England, he added a more serious first part, a savage attack on the state of criminal law (his special subject).

Wolsey and the king wanted him as part of their inner circle at court, and in 1529 he succeeded Wolsey as Lord Chancellor. Even his subtle legal mind could not save him from involvement in the king's divorce from Catherine of Aragon and marriage to Anne Boleyn. He refused to express a personal opinion, but was forced into increasingly open opposition to Henry and resigned as Chancellor after little more than three years. The loss of his position reduced him and his family to poverty. He refused to take the oath acknowledging Henry and Anne's children as heirs to the throne and was imprisoned in the Tower of London. Despite entreaties from his family and friends to reconcile himself with the king, he steadfastly upheld the supremacy of his conscience. He was eventually tried for treason, condemned (on false evidence) and executed

on 5 July 1535, famously declaring on the scaffold that he died 'the king's good servant and God's first'.

In 2000 Pope John Paul II declared him patron of statesmen and politicians, saying that he 'demonstrated in a singular way the value of a moral conscience'. There would seem to be ample scope for his example.

St Teresa of Avila

Founder and Doctor, 1515–82
15 October

Spanish Catholic writers; the Spanish Army Commissariat

Many saints are outstanding for achievement, and many are exceptionally lovable personalities; it would be difficult to find another who combined the two to such an extent as Teresa. Born into a wealthy Castilian family, she never seemed to relish the thought of marriage with its (then) subservient role for women and risk of early death from numerous births. Religious life apparently offered more freedom, and she joined the Carmelite Convent of the Incarnation outside Avila, where life, if not exactly worldly, was far from restrictive or harsh.

A near mortal illness was followed by a relatively unproductive decade, in which she, nevertheless, made gradual progress in mental prayer and began to envisage a different sort of community. This would be small, poor and strictly enclosed. Christ on the cross had nothing, she argued, so why should his dedicated followers have possessions? Overcoming objections from the Inquisition and others, she opened the first 'Discalced' (shoeless or barefoot) Carmelite convent in 1562.

Five years later she had thirteen nuns, living a life of poverty and penance purely on alms, but kept from gloom or self-abasement by Teresa's dislike of 'long-faced saints' (her face, luckily, being naturally round). The Carmelite general began to support her, and for nine years she travelled all over Spain making new foundations. As she went she wrote, producing a stream of letters illustrating her experiences, showing her good sense and down-to-earth character: 'God walks among the pots and pans' is one of her most typical comments. All the while, she herself was experiencing the heights of mystical union with God, which she described in books that have become classics, as has her autobiography.

Her reforms brought her determined opposition from the 'unreformed' Carmelites, who had her imprisoned and excommunicated her nuns. All women religious still had to belong to enclosed convents, and the papal nuncio called her a 'restless, disobedient and contumacious gad-about woman' who disobeyed St Paul. But King Philip II supported her, and gradually peace was established and the Discalced Carmelites were made into a separate province. She made more foundations, but her health, never robust, gave out, and she died trying to get back to Avila on 4 October 1582. She was immediately recognized as a saint, and was canonized with Ignatius,* the great male reformer of the age, in 1622. She was the first 'non-virgin-martyr' woman saint to have a feast-day in the universal

calendar, and Pope Paul VI declared her a Doctor of the Church in 1970.

Paul VI was also responsible, in 1965, for confirming her as patron of Spanish Catholic writers and, by extension, of all those with responsibility for the moral tone of publications. She became patron of the Spanish Army Commissariat (or Quartermaster's branch) four years earlier, perhaps on account of her care for everyday objects.

Emblems: pen and book, sometimes with a dove or an angel; a heart with rays and IHS monogram; a crucifix

St Rose of Lima

1586–1617

23 August

Central and South America, Peru, the Indies and the Philippines;
Peruvian nurses and armed forces; florists and gardeners

B orn to parents of Spanish descent, and therefore at the apex of the formal society that had developed in Lima several decades after the Spanish conquest, Rose was christened Isabel (Elizabeth) and got her nickname from her beauty, when a maid declared her to be like a rose. Destined by her parents for success in the marriage market, she was destined by her own formidable will for what she saw as service to God, which meant becoming a nun.

She set about frustrating her parents and suitors by methods derived from the biography of St Catherine of Siena,* rubbing her skin with lime and pepper to make herself as unattractive as possible. She also resorted to cutting herself and developed what we would now call bulimia. Like so many teenagers, but to an unusual degree, she obviously saw herself as trapped and misunderstood. Her parents refused to allow her to enter a convent, but their authority and position in society were diminished when they lost their money in a mining venture.

Rose decided to help them in her own way. She grew flowers in their garden and sold these. By this time she was living in a 'hermitage' she had built in the garden, wearing a crown of thorns and sleeping on broken tiles. She had visions in which Christ 'told' her that his cross had been yet more painful. She then turned a room in the family house into an infirmary and began nursing the sick. The ridicule that she had drawn changed to admiration, and she became extremely popular with the people.

Her life was inevitably short, and her treatment of her body took its final toll on 24 August 1617. She was immediately hailed as a saint, though not by the religious authorities, suspicious, as ever, of individual visionary experiences. But they had to bow to popular pressure, and she was canonized (with the great mystic St John of the Cross) in 1671. For some she will always be a deluded young woman and a thoroughly bad example; others might see her as a proto-feminist martyr to a patriarchal society. In Peru she is still widely popular and regarded as the founder of social services in the country.

Devotion to her in Peru led to her being declared its patron two years before she was canonized; this was then extended to the rest of Latin America and further afield. Her infirmary work led to her official patronage of Peruvian nurses in 1958; seven years later the armed forces of Peru asked for, and were granted, her special patronage. That of gardeners and florists remains unofficial, but is suitable enough, even if it suggests that gardening is more painful than it need be.

St Robert Bellarmine

Bishop and Doctor, 1542–621
17 September

Catechists and catechumens

Diminutive in stature and constantly in poor health, Robert Bellarmine possessed one the best minds of the Catholic Reformation carried out in response to the Protestant one, and he managed to live a long life crammed with pastoral as well as intellectual activity.

As a boy he learned to play the violin, compose good Latin verse, and take part in scholarly disputations. After attending a Jesuit school he determined to enter the Society of Jesus, doing so in Rome at the age of 18. He taught, preached and lectured during his ten years of study for the priesthood, teaching himself Greek to lecture on Demosthenes. He was ordained in Louvain in 1570 and spent the next seven years there, developing a 'controversial theology' designed to refute the Protestant Reformers. Because they relied so heavily on the Bible, Robert engaged in deep study of this, which included learning Hebrew. He did so to such effect that he wrote on Hebrew grammar.

He was recalled to Rome, where he preached and taught at the new Jesuit university, the Gregorianum. He developed his lectures into four large volumes of disputations, which immediately attracted widespread attention: the work was banned in Elizabethan England, but so many copies were smuggled in that a London bookseller claimed to have made more money out of

'this Jesuit' than out of 'all other divines'. He helped to revise St
Jerome's Vulgate Latin Bible, producing an edition that became
the standard one for over 400 years. His studies were interrupt-
ed when he was sent to try to resolve the dispute over the acces-
sion of the Protestant Henry of Navarre as king of France,
followed by three years as Jesuit provincial in Naples.

In 1597 Pope Clement VIII appointed him his personal theologian and asked him to write two catechisms, which also
became standard works for centuries. He was made a cardinal,
but lived on the food of the poor (bread and garlic), in an
unheated house from which he stripped the wall hangings to
clothe the poor. He was then appointed archbishop of Capua,
where he worked to reform the clergy and preached with his
usual zeal. Once more a new pope, Paul V, called him back to
Rome, making him Prefect of the Vatican library. He was still
involved in controversy: between Jesuits and Dominicans over the
nature of grace and free will, with King James I of England over
the divine right of kings and papal authority, and with his friend
Galileo over the theory that the earth revolved round the sun.

Toward the end of his life he began writing devotional
books, including an immensely popular *Art of Dying Well*. As his
health finally declined, streams of people came to see him for
the last time, but he had to wait until the
twentieth century for official recognition
as a saint (1930) and as a Doctor of the
Church (1931).

His patronage of those who instruct and
are instructed in the faith stems logically
from his life and work, but this, too, was
not made official until 1932.

St Francis de Sales

Bishop and Doctor, 1567–622
24 January

Journalists, editors, writers

B orn a quarter of a century after Robert Bellarmine* but dying just a year after him, this great bishop and writer is another of the towering figures of the Catholic Reformation. The intense spiritual friendship he formed with a young widow, known to us as St Jane Frances de Chantal, also sets him apart as one of the most attractive figures of the period.

His father wanted him to become a soldier or lawyer, but Francis, despite a brilliant doctorate in law from Padua University, was determined to be a priest and was already a famous preacher by the time he was ordained in 1593. The bishop of Geneva then gave him and his cousin Louis the arduous task of converting the poor and mountainous Chablais region back to Catholicism from the Calvinism that had claimed it. They laboured through all sorts of physical dangers for four years, with considerable success.

Travelling to Rome in 1598, he met Robert Bellarmine and the future Paul V. He planned, but abandoned, a vast 'Hostel for all the arts and sciences' in the Chablais region. In Paris he met King Francis I, who offered him a rich bishopric in France, to which he replied, 'Sire, I have married a poor wife [Geneva] and cannot desert her for a richer one.' He was then coadjutor bishop, but the bishop died and Francis took over, consecrated in 1602. His priority was to reform his diocese in line with the teachings of the Council of Trent, and his main weapons were preaching and letter writing.

Jeanne Frémyot had lost three children and then her husband, the baron de Chantal; she was being told by a confessor to see this as God's will and to do penance. Then she heard Francis preach and felt that a great weight had been lifted from her. Francis heard her general confession, told her that the previous advice was destroying her conscience, and so began one of the great friendships between saints. He decided she should found a new religious Congregation and wrote his treatise *On the Love of God* for one of its first nuns, Jeanne's cousin. They became known as the Order of the Visitation or Visitandines, and by 1635 had 65 houses in France.

Francis, meanwhile, had written his best-known book, *Introduction to the Devout Life*: aimed at lay people, it was hugely popular from the outset and soon translated into many languages. He was still busy visiting parishes, preaching to great crowds, and writing 20 or 30 letters every day. He was also sought as a counsellor in affairs of State and the wider Church, which involved journeys that eventually killed him. He managed a last meeting with Jane on his final journey and died after writing

HUMILITY three times on a piece of paper, in response to a nun's request for a final word of advice. He was canonized in 1655, with lengthy depositions from Jeanne helping his cause. He was declared a Doctor of the Church in 1877.

His patronage stems naturally from his work, which, besides books and letters, included a series of 'tracts' aimed at converting the inhabitants of the Chablais. It was confirmed by Pope Pius XI in 1923.

St Martin de Porres

Dominican lay brother, 1575–639
3 November

Persons of mixed race; social justice; Peruvian public education, public health and
television; Spanish trade unionists; barbers and hairdressers

Born to a Spanish father and a freed black slave mother in
Lima, Martin inherited his mother's features and his
father disowned him, though he did take care of his education.
He was then appointed governor of Panama and sent Martin
back to his mother. She practised herbal medicine and apprenticed him to a barber-surgeon. This made him proficient in
both traditional African and current Western medicine, which
was to stand him in good stead.

He was accepted as a Dominican lay brother, but full membership of the Order was denied to 'Indians, blacks and their
descendants'. He carried out menial tasks to pay for his board
and lodging, but also flung himself into every possible sort of
practical charity. His twofold medical knowledge enabled him
to effect some remarkable cures, which were soon being considered miraculous. He helped to set up an orphanage and a hospital for foundling children in Lima and was made responsible
for distributing food from the convent to the poor of the city.
The food seemed to multiply miraculously, and his reputation
as a wonder-worker further increased. His background gave
him a special sympathy for the plight of African slaves, made
to labour in dreadful conditions.

Describing himself as a poor mulatto and the property of

the Order, he offered himself in payment when his convent got into debt. He longed to be sent on a mission and martyred, but the Church at the time could see blacks only as recipients, not practitioners, of mission. In Peru, however, he overcame racial prejudice, and all colours and classes of society helped to carry him to his grave when he died at the age of 63. He had become not just 'the people's' saint but everyone's. The eurocentric Church, however, hesitated over declaring his sanctity, and he was beatified only in 1837 and canonized in 1962 when, with the opening of the Second Vatican Council, the Catholic Church truly began to see itself as universal.

His patronage of persons of mixed race derives from his own ancestry, and its roots are traditional. He was declared patron of work for social justice by Pius XII, at the request of the Peruvian hierarchy, in 1935. Thirty years later, Paul VI made him patron of public education in Peru, which the bishops saw as including mass instruction in the faith through television. His patronage of Spanish trade unionists (then the 'national syndicate for various trades') was confirmed in 1973, and of Peruvian public health workers by John Paul II in 1982. Barbers, formerly barber-surgeons, developed into hairdressers as medicine became the preserve of doctors, and he was made patron of Italian hairdressers at their request in 1966.

St John-Francis Régis

Jesuit priest, 1597–640
31 December

Marriage; natural-born children; social workers, especially medical social workers

T he Council of Trent (1545–63) set in motion a process of re-Christianizing the rural areas of Europe, relatively neglected during centuries of 'cultural' Catholicism and then reduced to virtual paganism by religious wars. In south-central and south-western France, many areas had been won over to Calvinism in the aftermath of the Reformation, but then both Calvinists and Catholics had become progressively more ignorant of their faith, deprived of instruction by brigand nobles and absentee ministers and priests. It was such situations that the Jesuits and other Orders set out to redress.

John-Francis, educated by the Jesuits in the region, was marked out by his superior as a future saint from an early date and, after his ordination in 1631, spent what remained of his life preaching missions in remote areas. He had the sense to see that peasants needed to spend their summers working on the harvest, so he preached in towns then and in villages in the winters. The area he covered is harsh and mountainous, and he travelled on remote tracks in all weathers, once spending three weeks sleeping in a snowdrift.

His message was mainly for the poor, the sick and the needy of all sorts, but it was expressed with such sincerity that the wealthier and more educated people also flocked to hear him, so that he was often preaching to crowds of several thousand.

He had a special concern for trying to rescue prostitutes from their way of life (generally enforced by poverty) and for establishing refuges for what we would now call abused wives: both these concerns aroused opposition, mainly from the abusers, but popular support always enabled him to continue.

After some years in the more southerly part of his region he was asked by the bishop of Viviers to help in his particularly remote and deprived diocese, and here he spent his final years, spending his last four summers in the town of Le Puy and his winters in the surrounding villages. The toll on his health was too heavy, and by the autumn of 1640 he knew his end was approaching. He reached the town of La Louvesc, struggled through giving an Advent retreat, preached three times on Christmas Day and again on Boxing Day, but then succumbed to pleurisy and died on New Year's Eve. He was canonized in 1737. It was a pilgrimage to John-Francis' shrine that convinced St John Vianney* of his vocation about a century later.

He is traditionally patron of marriage and married people because his work with prostitutes was seen as strengthening the institution of marriage; in the same way his concern for couples in 'irregular' unions extended to the education of their children, so he became their patron too. His care of the sick also traditionally became a patronage of those who work for them.

St Jean de Brébeuf and Companions

Martyrs, died between 1642 and 1649

19 October

Canada

The French were the first to colonize territory in what is now Canada – 'New France' to them – early in the seventeenth century. Samuel Champlain founded Quebec in 1608; Franciscan missionaries soon followed, and they called on the Jesuits for help. Two sailed in 1613, but were driven back by English pirates. A further four, including Brébeuf, arrived in 1625. In 1630 the English blockaded the St Lawrence River and forced Champlain and the missionaries out, but Champlain challenged the legitimacy of this seizure in the London law courts and won, so Canada reverted to French control in 1632.

Jean de Brébeuf joined the Jesuit novitiate in Rouen in 1617, was ordained around 1622, and become bursar of the Jesuit college. His health was considered so frail that he was restricted to a two-year teaching course, but he somehow survived many years of extreme hardship and ill treatment in North America before his eventual appalling martyrdom in 1649. He spent his first winter living with Algonquin Indians: sleeping in tepees filled with squaws, dogs, fleas and smoke, hunting with the men by day and starving when they did. After five months he was able to compose a short grammar and dictionary of their language.

The following summer he went, by canoe where possible, carrying everything overland where not, to the land of the Hurons. His two companions left, and he struggled on alone, becoming 'the Sorcerer' when he prayed for rain and it fell. He was forced back to France with Champlain in 1630, and took his final vows there, returning to New France in 1633. He stayed a further three years among the Hurons, who were subject to attacks of increasing ferocity by the Iroquois, forcing him to move the mission several times. During these years he began sending back detailed accounts of his travels and experiences: known as the 'Jesuit Relations'; these accounts soon aroused intense interest all over Europe.

Martyrdom was becoming increasingly probable and the Jesuits expressed their desire for it in their 'Relations'. A lay medical assistant was tomahawked to death in 1642. This was followed by the first Jesuit death, that of Isaac Jogues, two years later, with a new assistant killed the next day. In July 1648 Fr Antoine Daniel was shot by arrows and thrown into his chapel, which was set on fire, and in March the following year Brébeuf and Fr Gabriel Lalemant were captured by Iroquois, tortured with unbelievable savagery, and finally killed. Fr Charles Garnier and an assistant were killed in December 1649. The eight were canonized as the Proto-Martyrs of North America in 1930, and their joint feast-day on 19 October was established and extended to the universal Church in 1969.

They are obvious choices as patrons of Canada because they died in an effort to convert its peoples; the patronage was officially confirmed in 1940.

St Vincent de Paul

Founder, 1581–660
27 September

Madagascar; charities; hospitals; prisoners

Vincent, whom the film *Monsieur Vincent* was to make one of the best-known saints of all time, trained for the priesthood with Franciscans in Gascony and was ordained at the young age of just 19, after which he studied theology at Toulouse. He went to Rome, but for how long is a mystery, as he seems to have muddied the history of several years with a series of letters describing his seizure by pirates and captivity in Tunisia, which he apparently invented, for reason or reasons unknown.

Back in Paris he joined the new Congregation of the Oratory, and after a spell as a parish priest was appointed tutor to the eldest son of the powerful Gondi family, staying in this post for twelve years. He was not cut off from the general lot of poor people, as he ministered to the peasants on the Gondi estates. He came to see the need for long-term care of those who suffered misfortune, over and above immediate assistance, and brought together a group of women who would take turns to look after the sick poor, devising a Rule for them.

He then formed a group of priests whose special mission would be to preach in villages, which he extended to caring for the poor and for convicts. They lived in common and became known as Vincentians, or Lazarists, from their new headquarters in the priory of Saint-Lazare. Their success prompted the archbishop of Paris to ask Vincent to help in training his diocesan clergy, and this led to Saint-Lazare becoming one of the great centres for church reform in France. His 'Ladies of Charity' began to find some tasks beneath their dignity or beyond their strength, and Vincent asked his closest helper, Louise de Marillac, to find simple country girls to help them. Their numbers grew, and he found himself with another group that needed an organized basis. To avoid the need for enclosure, then enjoined on all women religious, he avoided permanent vows, and the Sisters of Charity, as they became known, still make private vows each year.

For 27 years he gave weekly conferences, which had a huge impact on the training of young priests, while his Vincentians gave equally influential courses in seminaries. He founded hospitals for the old, the sick, for foundlings and for galley slaves. He was called to King Louis XIII on his deathbed and became a counsellor to the queen regent, Anne of Austria. He was partly responsible for the condemnation of five basic Jansenist propositions by the pope: a condemnation that he hoped – largely in vain – would be accepted in a spirit of charity. He died peacefully at Saint-Lazare and was canonized in 1737. His Vincentians and Sisters of Charity still work all over the world, joined by the lay Society of St Vincent de Paul.

His patronages stem obviously from his life's work. That of charities was formally proclaimed by Pope Leo XIII in 1885. He is patron of Madagascar because he sent missionaries there (as well as to Poland, Ireland, Scotland and North Africa); this was recognized in 1949 and 1961.

St Joseph of Copertino

Franciscan friar, 1603–63
18 September

Students, exam candidates; aviators, astronauts

Joseph, with St Gerard Majella,* is something of an exception in this selection in that he is someone who apparently did little but to whom extraordinary things were done. Whatever explanation one gives – faith, miracle, diabolic possession – many saints have displayed physical phenomena that contradict the known laws of nature, and none to a greater degree than Joseph of Copertino.

Born in a shed, as his father had had to sell their house to pay debts, Joseph was a vague and forgetful child, known as *Bocaperta* (Gaper), because of his tendency to wander around with his mouth open. Despite his lack of education, he was determined to enter the religious life: the Franciscans refused him; the Capuchins accepted him and then threw him out; then the Franciscans took him on as a tertiary and set him to work in a stable, which delighted him. They then accepted him as a novice and eventually allowed him to be ordained.

He took to eating very little and doing severe penances, which seems to have lightened his body as well as his spirit, as he developed the 'gift' of levitation, rising from the ground, often in front of quite sober and independent witnesses. One example was when the wife of the Spanish ambassador to Naples asked to meet him: as he came into the church, he was whisked over her head to the feet of a statue of Our Lady, where he prayed for a moment and then came back down. The ambassador called him another St Francis,* to which the pope replied that one was enough.

The gift, and the fame it brought him, in fact ruined his outward life, as he became an embarrassment to the friars, who sent him away to remote places, forbade him to say Mass, and generally treated him with a complete lack of understanding. All of this made him feel unworthy, and the intervention of the Inquisition, which transferred him to the Capuchins, who kept him in virtual solitary confinement for three or four years, made things worse. He was eventually returned to the Franciscans, who treated him only slightly better until his death. He was immediately acclaimed by the people as a saint, but the Church was, as usual, far more cautious, eventually canonizing him over a century after his death, and then on account of his exceptional humility, gentleness and patience, not for the physical phenomena – rather as Bernadette was later to be canonized for her life as a nun and not for the apparitions at Lourdes.

He is traditionally the patron of students and exam candidates because of the extreme difficulty he experienced (and over-

came) in learning. His patronage of aviators and then astronauts is for splendidly obvious reasons, and a good example of the need for a patron still being felt in modern times.

St John Baptist de La Salle

Founder, 1651–719
7 April

Schoolteachers

J ohn Baptist's early life gave little indication that he was to become a great educator of poor children. Wealthy and aristocratic, he became a canon of Reims Cathedral and seemed destined for a career of comfortable advancement in the Church.

Then in 1679 he was asked to help open a free school for poor children. This request was put to him by a layman named Adrian Nyel, who had opened such schools in Rouen. John Baptist soon found himself engrossed in what he had supposed would be merely an administrative task. He even took some teachers into the family home in order to train them better, whereupon most of the family decamped in horror at this intrusion of the unwashed. He took the teachers away, found them a rented house, gave all his money to charity and resigned from being a cathedral canon.

He planned an organization, of religious but not priests, dedicated to providing free Christian education. He and twelve teachers formed themselves into the 'Brothers of the Christian Schools' (not to be confused with the later, Irish, Christian Brothers) and were soon opening new schools, despite opposition from those running fee-paying Catholic schools. They needed a Rule to be recognized as a religious Congregation, and John Baptist composed one, setting the aim as achieving holiness through total dedication to teaching. He followed this with a series of books on what he saw as the principles of Catholic education.

All that he wrote about education was based on the practice of his Brothers. He encouraged 'whole-class' teaching, careful planning of the curriculum and frequent testing – all modern concepts well ahead of his time. His more general observations on the Christian life stemmed from his own aristocratic background and would not have seemed appropriate to the poor to whom his teaching methods were directed, though he was equally in advance of his time in encouraging frequent Communion.

James II of England was exiled to France in 1688, and his Catholic Irish followers asked the Brothers to educate their children. Some of these were older than those they had previously taught, so they moved into secondary education. Opposition continued from clerics and lay schoolmasters in Paris, so John Baptist moved the congregation's headquarters to Rouen, where they opened a boarding school and later a reformatory, which went on to become their speciality.

In 1714 John Baptist was forcibly elected superior-general, but three years later he was allowed to move into semi-retirement, spending the next five years writing, meditating and living very humbly according to what he saw as God's direct will. He died on Good Friday of 1719. His Brothers were suppressed by the French Revolution, but enjoyed a massive revival in the nine-teenth century and still work worldwide.

John Baptist, finally canonized in 1900, was declared principal patron of all who teach young people by Pope Pius XII in 1950, an obvious choice based on his life and work.

St Gerard Majella

1726–55
16 October

Mothers

After St Joseph of Copertino,* Gerald is probably the best-known example of levitation and bilocation among saints, but St Joseph became the patron of fliers, while Gerald became unofficially that of mothers, for reasons that may or may not be connected with his life, which lasted a mere 29 years before he succumbed to tuberculosis.

Born south of Naples, he was apprenticed to a tailor, where he was bullied by his co-workers. He then became a servant in a bishop's household, but the bishop proved even more of a bully, so he returned home and worked as a tailor, supporting his widowed mother and his sisters. He tried to join the Capuchins, but they decided he was too young and not strong enough. Eventually, in 1752, the Redemptorists admitted him as a lay brother – their founder, St Alphonsus de'Liguori,* seeing qualities in him that others failed to see. He was soon helping Redemptorist priests in their principal task of preaching missions and showed a real gift for seeing into people's hearts and encouraging them to repent of their sins.

He went into ecstatic trances, during some of which he rose into the air – on one occasion, according to witnesses, flying for half a mile before coming back to earth. He was also 'seen' in two places at once – attending to a sick cottager while talking to a friend in his monastery, for example. (This phenome-

non of 'bilocation' can often be a picturesque way of saying
that a person achieves so much that he/she appears to be
everywhere at once.) His reputation for holiness and miracle
working spread like wildfire – in a supposedly sceptical and
'enlightened' century (though perhaps less so around Naples) –
with more people coming to see him than the monastery could
cope with, so he was moved. For the short time remaining to
him, he seemed to conjure food and clothes for beggars out of
nowhere. He died exactly when he had foretold he would, and
was canonized in 1904.

The second centenary of his death, 1955, saw a worldwide peti-
tion for his patronage to be extended to all women, in what
might be seen as a pre-feminist popular devotion. What made
him appeal so much to women? Perhaps the fact that he
worked at sewing; or that he looked after his widowed mother;
or that he was physically weak and was bullied and died young;

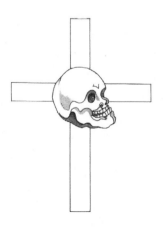

or that his gift of bilocation is exactly what busy women, especially mothers, need: 'I can't be in two places at once, you know!'

There is another possible explanation: devotion to him produced many popular representations of the prayer-card variety, and in some he is shown with a skull and a cross. In Central American Voodoo, an underworld figure who protects women in childbirth also carries these symbols. In the American melting-pot of popular Catholicism and former African religions, symbols such as these move both ways.

St Alphonsus de'Liguori

Bishop, founder and Doctor, 1696–787

1 August

Confessors; moral theologians

Alphonsus was the eldest son of the captain of galleys in what was then the Spanish kingdom of Naples. A brilliant student, he held a doctorate in law by the age of 16 and practised law for eight years. Losing a dispute over land after an unbroken run of success, he saw this as a sign from God, gave up practising law and any thought of marrying, and joined the Oratory.

He was ordained in 1726 and began preaching missions throughout the kingdom. As a preacher, he was effective without being bombastic or overdoing the prospect of hellfire. A friendship with another priest and an encounter with a visionary Visitandine nun led to his founding a new Congregation for men, to be devoted to bringing the faith to the poor of Naples. This was the Congregation of the Most Holy Redeemer, generally known as Redemptorists. It obtained ecclesiastical approval and operated through the preaching of missions, which soon spread beyond Naples to rural areas. Alphonsus himself preached such missions for 26 years.

He also applied his fine mind to the study of moral theology and published an extremely successful book on the subject. His approach was subtle and gave rise to the technical term of 'probabilism'. He also wrote a book on Mary, which remained highly influential in spreading devotion to her for well over a hundred years. His motive in writing this was partly to oppose the rigorous Jansenist movement, which decried the value of such devotion. He was able to devote more time to writing from 1752, when declining health obliged him to be less active as head of the Congregation, but he still had many more years of work before him.

In 1762 the pope appointed him bishop of Sant'Agata dei Goti, a diocese from which effective religion had virtually disappeared. He organized missions, using priests from other Orders to prevent claims of favouritism, and set about reforming the clergy. He sold all he had to bring relief in time of plague and famine. Despite suffering from rheumatic fever and attacks from other quarters in the Church, he soldiered on until 1775. His last years were marred by betrayal over forms of the Redemptorist Rule, when he was tricked into signing a version for approval by the civil authorities in Naples that was a travesty of the true Rule, which had been already approved by the pope. He found himself cut off from his own Order and went through a terrible 'dark night of the soul', from which he recovered some months before his death. He was canonized in 1839 and made a Doctor of the Church in 1871.

His patronages derive from his magisterial work on moral theology, which gave confessors far more freedom to judge the severity of sins than they had previously possessed.

St John Vianney

1786–859

4 August

Parish priests

The priest known the world over as the 'Curé d'Ars', whose extraordinary popularity eventually earned him high honours from Church and State, had unpropitious beginnings. Born into a peasant family, he caused them hardship by insisting on studying for the priesthood rather than working on the land. He was a poor student, finding Latin very difficult. He was mistakenly drafted into the army and inadvertently became a deserter for a year, forced to hide until an amnesty freed him in 1810.

At the major seminary in Lyons, instruction was in Latin, and he quite failed to keep up. A perceptive vicar-general nevertheless saw his obvious goodness as more important than learning and allowed him to be ordained. After a period as curate to the priest who had taught him at his first school, he was appointed parish priest of Ars-en-Dombe. He set about converting this mean and semi-pagan little village to a life focused wholly on religion. He banned the sale of alcohol, dancing and swearing, forced the villagers to keep Sundays for Mass and Vespers, preached assiduously and spent long hours in the confessional.

Gradually, as news of the changes spread, so too did his fame, and he was revered by many and hated by others – including, he believed, the devil, who sent alarming poltergeist-type manifestations to harry him, even setting his bed on fire. Two women opened a free school in the village, and this became a shelter for all who needed it, the focus of such charity that its provision could only be seen as miracles worked by the priest, though he attributed it to St Philomena (now seen as unhistorical), to whom he had a great devotion.

The number of pilgrims to Ars grew exponentially, so that the railway station in Lyons had to open a special ticket office to cope with the numbers. Vianney was forced to spend ever longer hearing confessions – up to sixteen hours a day in summer. He undoubtedly had an exceptional facility for seeing into people's minds and did not hesitate to speak his mind, telling a future nun who wanted some relics to make them herself. And all the time he really wanted to be a monk; three times he ran away to become one, but each time he was sent back by the bishop.

By the 1850s, over a thousand pilgrims a week were flocking to Ars, and the strain on him became too great. He had been made an honorary canon, but sold the cape that was the mark of rank; he was also made a knight of the Legion of Honour, but never wore the insignia. He was still hearing Confessions on his deathbed. He had achieved a phenomenal success on his terms and set a pattern for priests, with emphasis on private Confession and strict morality, that largely defined Catholic parish life for at least a century. He was canonized in 1925.

Most unusually, he was declared patron of French parish priests twenty years before being canonized. This was extended to parish priests worldwide four years after his canonization.

St Antony Mary Claret

Founder, 1807–70
24 October

Weavers; savings banks

T he son of a weaver from Catalonia, Antony worked at his father's trade, as well as studying printing, before entering a seminary. He was ordained diocesan priest in 1835, but his heart was set on joining a religious Order. He became a Jesuit novice in Rome, but his precarious health forced him to leave the Society.

Returning to Catalonia, he preached missions and retreats for ten years. He had a great devotion to the Immaculate Heart of Mary and in 1849 founded a Congregation of priests dedicated to spreading this devotion. They became known as Claretians, for his surname. He put his knowledge of printing to good use and, using the new powered printing presses, issued a steady stream of pamphlets and books, including the 'Religious Library', with five million copies of its books and booklets printed in twenty years.

In 1850 he was, to his consternation, appointed archbishop of Santiago in Cuba. Once there, he set about a thorough reform of a neglected archdiocese. He made three complete visitations of the territory, set up new parishes, visited hospitals, and attended personally to victims of disasters. He also established a savings bank with a branch in every parish. After seven years, he was recalled as abruptly as he had been appointed, to act as confessor to Queen Isabella II of Spain.

Life at court hardly suited his nature, given as it was to endless travel and new initiatives. But as the court moved around Spain, he found fresh outlets for his energies: he founded the Congregation of Catholic Mothers and established religious libraries to educate the laity; as rector of the Royal Monastery of the Escorial he established a laboratory, a natural history museum, and music and language schools; he founded an academy to promote the apostolate of Christian writing; and he imposed extra and severe penances on his own life.

His association with the ultra-clerical and conservative monarchy of Isabella was turned against him when she was forced off the throne by the liberal revolution of 1868. The Spanish Claretian houses were closed, and his priests took refuge in France, but he was further hounded by anti-clericals and not even allowed to stay with them. He was even accused of trying to procure weapons to overthrow the liberal Spanish government, but nothing could be proved by the time of his death. He was canonized in 1950, and the Claretians carry on his missionary apostolate through publishing, including their *Christian Community Bible*, published in many languages from their base in the Philippines.

Neither of his patronages has been officially confirmed, but both are well established and stem from his early life and his actions as archbishop respectively.

St John Bosco

Founder, 1815–88
31 January

Mexican young people; editors; apprentices

'D on' Bosco, as he was everywhere known, lived through a time of rapid change in society, brought about largely by the impact of industrialization. In his city of Turin, this produced an underclass of young people looking for work: homeless and beyond the reach of the parish system.

Ordained in 1841, Don Bosco began to dedicate himself to their care. He had to contend with an anticlerical government that suppressed all religious houses, and he got round this law by collecting abandoned boys into what he called an 'Oratory'. Starting with six, the number of boys in his care soon grew to over 800. He developed a 'total dedication' approach to his charges: every aspect of their lives was to be under constant supervision. He opened workshops where they could learn trades — tailor, shoemaker, joiner, printer, bookbinder, iron foundry worker.

He was accused of undercutting the 'professionals' and of subverting the parish system, but the movement grew, with other priests coming to join him, so forming what was to become the Salesian (after St Francis de Sales*) Congregation. His practical approach proved its worth during a cholera epidemic, when he volunteered his boys to care for the sick and remove dead bodies. Not one of them died, which was regarded as miraculous, but was due more to his instructions that they wash their hands in vinegar. Even the government came to respect him to the extent of allowing his Congregation to form, despite the general ban.

He found time to write histories, biographies and popular textbooks of religious instruction. He was the first saint to undergo a press interview, at which he shrugged off suggestions of being a miracle worker, saying that he simply did what Jesus and Mary enabled him to do. He was also the first to exhibit at a major exhibition when he took a stand at the 1884 National Exhibition of Industry, Science and Art, where visitors were astonished at his professional presentation of the complete process of book production. By the time he died, the Salesians were working all over Europe and in America. He was canonized in 1934 and the following day was declared a national holiday in Italy.

He was declared patron of Mexican young people in 1935; of Catholic editors in 1946; and of apprentices in Italy, Colombia and Spain in 1958, 1959 and 1960 (respectively), reflecting his work with young people.

St Thérèse of Lisieux

Carmelite nun and Doctor of the Church, 1873–97
1 October

Missions; France; florists and flower growers

This most popular saint of modern times, now recognized as a spiritual genius who made a truly original contribution to Christian life, was born in Normandy. When she was only four, her mother died. She found a second mother in her eldest sister, Pauline, but Pauline joined the Carmelites in Lisieux when Thérèse was nine, leaving her bereft once more.

She longed to follow Pauline and a second sister, Marie, into the convent and, after an initial rejection on the grounds of her age, was allowed to do so when she was 15. There she developed her 'little way', carrying out the meanest task to perfection for the greater glory of God. This had nothing childish about it: her perception of herself as a 'little soul' was designed to combat pride. She was well acquainted with the great Carmelite mystics and other masters, and developed her teaching quite consciously, eventually ordering it into autobiographical form in *The Story of a Soul.*

Life in the convent was hard in many ways, made worse by doubts about her vocation and family troubles outside. Her father died in 1894 after spending three years in an institution after a series of strokes, releasing another sister, Céline, to join the convent. Thérèse became assistant novice-mistress, her only official post. She took to writing plays and poems to celebrate convent occasions, and her letters are numerous and vivid. Her interest in missions was aroused by reading the life and letters of Blessed Théophane Vénard, martyred in Indo-China (Vietnam) in 1861, and she tried to move to the convent in Hanoi.

This was prevented by the first signs of the tuberculosis that was to render her last years a long process of worsening physical suffering, accompanied toward the end by a real 'dark night of the soul', during which she saw heaven, previously so longed-for, as a source of pain and conflict. After eighteen months of acute suffering unrelieved by drugs or oxygen, she died on 30 September 1897. She had expressed a determination to 'spend my heaven doing good upon earth' (as she wrote to a missionary in Vietnam), and as her popularity grew, so did cures attributed to her intercession. She was beatified in 1923 and canonized in 1925.

Her image circulated in millions of sentimentalized prints, but later publication of untouched photographs has revealed a much stronger face, in keeping with the inner toughness of her teaching, recognized by her proclamation as Doctor of the Church in her centenary year, 1997.

Because of her concern for missions, she was proclaimed their principal patron two years after her canonization. She officially

joined St Joan of Arc* as a 'second patron' of France in 1944, when France itself was seen as mission territory. Her writings contain an elaborate code of references to flowers, and she referred to herself as 'the little flower', which has led to her traditional patronage of florists and flower growers.

St Frances Xavier Cabrini

Founder, 1850–917
22 December

Emigrants, migrants

T he fact that there is only one saint in this selection who died in the twentieth century does not indicate that this century produced no saints: it did, many and some great ones, mostly martyrs produced by totalitarian regimes, but they are not so far recognized as patrons: a process, whether by popular acclaim or official decree, that takes time. 'Mother' Cabrini could hardly be a more appropriate patron, in view of current world conditions, to close this selection of saints who are patrons because of their real achievements, not just through popular stories attached to their names.

Named after St Francis Xavier,* Frances tried to become a missionary in China, literally following in his footsteps, but was rejected by two Orders on account of her tiny stature and frail health. So she set about founding a new Congregation devoted to missions. This was before St Thérèse,* and the Church did not accept the idea of women being missionaries. Her Sacred Heart Sisters, approved in 1880, had to work in Italy for the time being.

Italy was in the grip of mass emigration, mainly to the USA, as a way out of its endemic poverty. In the USA, Italians collected in ghettoes, were exploited by employers, lost to the Church and uncared for by the State. Frances happened to meet their great champion, Bishop (now Blessed) John Baptist

Scalabrini, who saw how useful her Sisters could be. Pope Leo XIII confirmed that they could finally go overseas, 'not to the east, but to the west'.

With six other Sisters, she sailed to New York, where they found no welcome (as the archbishop did not agree with women missionaries) and had to rent a slum tenement. Gradually, they won through to the poor and sick, and their obvious devotion brought increasing contributions as Italian immigrants began to improve their financial lot. Then wealthy Americans began to offer houses, and the work spread. She saw her Sisters as teachers, but she was persuaded to open a hospital in New York. From there her mission spread, and she travelled to Central and South America, making the same provision for Italian immigrants there. She returned often to Italy to recruit more Sisters and opened houses in France and Spain to provide Sisters whose native languages would be understood. She became a naturalized citizen of the USA in 1907, and is known as its 'first citizen saint'. She collapsed and died suddenly just before Christmas 1917, and was canonized in 1946.

She was proclaimed patron of emigrants by Pope Pius XII in 1950, by which time she was already called 'mother of emigrants'.

Glossary of terms used

BEATIFICATION Declaration by the papacy that a candidate for canonization has met the requirements and is to be referred to as 'Blessed' (Latin *beatus* or *beata*). Many remain Blessed for long periods, possibly forever.

BLESSED Title accorded to those for whom a declaration of beatification has been made by the pope, entitling them to veneration but not enforcing it.

CANONIZATION Declaration of a person's sainthood and entitlement to obligatory veneration. The final stage in the process of making saints, reserved to the papacy since about 1200, before which sainthood, involving the inclusion of a feast-day in the calendar was a local decision in response to popular demand.

DOCTOR (OF THE CHURCH) Title conferred since the Middle Ages on the saints who have made a significant theological contribution.

EMBLEM Pictorial device used to identify a saint, usually based on an element in his/her life.

LIFE Used with a capital letter denotes a written account. Some Lives are genuine, some legendary and based on earlier examples.

MIRACLE Popularly, an event for which no natural explanation can be found and which is therefore attributed to divine intervention. In the context of sainthood, one 'miracle' is, with rare exceptions, still required for beatification, and another for canonization. These are normally inexplicable cures, worked after the candidate's death.

PATRON(AGE) See Introduction.

RULE With a capital, denotes a written guide, officially approved as embodying the way of life to be followed by members of religious Orders.

SAINT(S) Those recognized by the Church as having gained the reward of heaven and suitable to be venerated and followed as examples on earth.